THE COMPLETE BOOK
OF PALMISTRY

About the Author

Richard Webster was born in New Zealand in 1946, where he still resides. He travels widely every year, lecturing and conducting workshops on psychic subjects around the world. He has written many books, mainly on psychic subjects, and also writes monthly magazine columns. Richard is married with three children. His family is very supportive of his occupation, but his oldest son, after watching his father's career, has decided to become an accountant.

Many of Llewellyn's authors have websites with additional information and resources. For more information, please visit our website at www.llewellyn.com.

THE COMPLETE BOOK OF
PALMISTRY

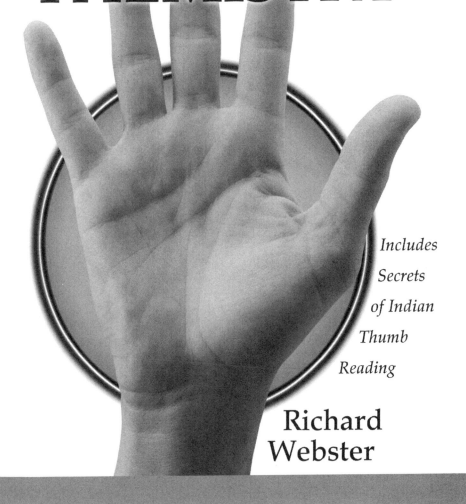

Includes

Secrets

of Indian

Thumb

Reading

Richard
Webster

2001

Llewellyn Publications

St. Paul, Minnesota 55164-0383, U.S.A.

Second Edition
First Printing, 2001
(Previously titled *Revealing Hands*)

Book design and editing by Kimberly Nightingale
Cover photo © 2001 by Digital Stock
Cover design by Gavin Dayton Duffy
Interior illustrations by Carla Shale

Library of Congress Cataloging-in-Publication Data

Webster, Richard, 1946-
     The complete book of palmistry : includes secrets of
Indian thumb reading / Richard
Webster.—2nd ed.
     p. cm.
Rev. ed. of: Revealing hands. c1994.
Includes bibliographical references (p.) and index.
ISBN 1-56718-790-0
     1. Palmistry.   I. Webster, Richard, 1946-Revealing
hands. II. Title.

BF921 .W399 2001
133.6—dc21   2001029206

Llewellyn Publications
A Division of Llewellyn Worldwide, Ltd.
P.O. Box 64383, Dept. 1-56718-790-0
St. Paul, MN 55164-0383, U.S.A.
www.llewellyn.com

Printed in the United States of America

For Margaret,
the special person in my life,
and for our children
Nigel, Charlotte, and Philip

Other Books by Richard Webster

Astral Travel for Beginners
Aura Reading for Beginners
Dowsing for Beginners
Feng Shui for Beginners
Llewellyn Feng Shui series
Numerology Magic
Omens, Oghams & Oracles
101 Feng Shui Tips for the Home
Palm Reading for Beginners
Seven Secrets to Success
Soul Mates
Spirit Guides and Angel Guardians
Success Secrets

Forthcoming

Practical Guide to Past-Life Memories
Write Your Own Magic

TABLE OF CONTENTS

FOREWORD

PALMISTRY HAS BEEN an obsession of mine since I was a young child. I must have travelled well over a hundred thousand miles over the years in my quest for information. I have spoken with palmists all around the world, and learned something from almost all of them. Hopefully, they learned from me, as well. I have also learned a great deal from my students. There is a saying that the teacher teaches what he most needs to know, and that has certainly been true in my case. I have more than three hundred books on palmistry in my library, and still buy new books on the subject whenever they appear, in the hope that I will learn something new. Every now and again, I do.

Different cultures have different ways of doing things. For instance, palmistry is much more fatalistic in the Far East than it is in the West. Palmists in the East frequently predict accidents and other disasters for their clients. Some even tell people when they are going to die. Needless to say, advice of this sort can become a self-fulfilling prophecy that proves how accurate the palmist was. In Asia, palmists assume that your main interest in life is money, and frame their readings accordingly. In the West, palmistry is being used more and more for character analysis, career guidance, and health. In fact, I believe that the greatest breakthroughs yet to come with palmistry involve health matters. However, despite these differences in approach, the fundamentals of palmistry are the same everywhere.

Although my two books on the subject are intended for interested beginners, I approached each one differently, both in what was or was not included, and also in the depth of material included. For instance, in this book I have included a chapter on the degrees of the hand. This does not appear in the second book, not because I did not think it was important, but because I considered other topics to be more valuable for the beginner. Knowledge of the degrees of the hand is useful because it allows you to make assessments at a glance, even when not actually reading the person's hands.

I have also included sample scripts in this book. This is because not everyone has access to an experienced palm reader. The scripts enable you to see exactly what a palm reader would say when presented with a certain line or mark on a person's hand. Although this was intended to help people who were just becoming interested in the subject, I have received numerous letters from more advanced students who found the scripts helpful when starting to give serious readings.

Palmistry is growing and developing all the time. I have met many people around the world who are researching different aspects of the subject. There are still many aspects of palmistry in which you can make valuable and original contributions.

Health and career are two notable examples. It would be hard to think of a topic more important than health, and a great deal of research is going on into determining health factors in the palms of the hand. Researchers are scientifically proving things that palmists have known about for hundreds, even thousands, of years. One example is determing people's predispositions to different illnesses.

Another important area is in finding the right careers for people. Many people have no idea what they want to do with their lives. A good palmist can suggest careers that will best utilize their particular talents and interests. I have included a chapter on careers in this book.

One area of particular interest to me is dermatoglyphics. This is overlooked in many books on palmistry. However, as it provides valuable insights into the person's makeup that cannot be learned in any other way, I consider it highly valuable. There is a complete chapter on dermatoglyphics in this book.

Palmistry has been a lifelong interest of mine, and I am still learning. I will never know everything about palmistry as there is so much to it. This excites me, as I quickly lose interest in subjects which have little depth to them. That is not the case with palmistry.

I have spent a great deal of time in India, and felt that I had learned most of what Indian palmistry had to offer. A few years ago, I was fortunate enough to spend a few days with a good friend of mine in New Delhi. Sameer Upadhyay is not only an old friend and an excellent host, he is also an exceptional palm reader, with a gentle, caring, and understanding way with his clients. During my stay he kindly taught me his system of reading thumbs.

Many palmists in India read only the thumb, but it has taken me up until now to find anyone who would tell me about it. This information has never appeared in English before, and I am thrilled to be able to include it here. Thumb reading is another area where original research can still be done. I do not have the time to do this myself, at least at present. Maybe you will have the time and the interest. It is an exciting prospect to think that you may discover valuable insights that will help future generations of palmists.

I hope this book enthuses and inspires you. Palmistry is a wonderful, incredibly useful talent. You will derive enormous satisfaction from helping people navigate their way through life. Your popularity will soar, and countless people will benefit from your knowledge and expertise. Palmistry is one of my passions. I hope it also becomes one of yours.

INTRODUCTION

Many books on palmistry seem to have been written with the intent of confusing the reader. This one is different. It is designed to take you step by step through every aspect of palm reading from the basics to the more involved areas.

Wherever possible I have included a script that can be used when describing a particular feature on the hand. This enables you to make comments about other people's hands within a few minutes of starting the book. The script is not intended to be memorized, but to let you know what a palmist is likely to say when confronted with a certain line or marking on a palm. As something on one part of the hand can contradict something shown elsewhere, these scripts are meant to be used as a guide only. They are also intended to give you some confidence as you start your study of this fascinating subject.

I have been interested in palmistry for almost all of my life. As a ten-year-old I remember sitting in a large overstuffed chair in the library of a neighbor's house fascinated with his talk about palmistry, whilst eating his wife's cake and scones. I was a keen reader and it was their library that intrigued me initially. No one else I had met until then had a special room devoted entirely to books, and his books were so different. He had a huge section devoted to palmistry and I loved the names of the authors: Desbarolles, D'Arpentigny, Cheiro, and Benham. Amused at my growing interest, my neighbor started teaching me the basics of palmistry, and gradually the palmistry lessons became more important than the food his wife produced in such copious quantities. They were a childless, middle-aged couple and obviously enjoyed my visits. One Christmas they gave me a copy of the 1895 edition of Captain D'Arpentigny's *The Science of the Hand*, translated by Ed Heron-Allen, still one of my most cherished possessions. Sadly for me they finally moved away, but the seed had been sown.

I have carried on with my studies for more than thirty years since then. I have been fortunate enough to learn from palmists in many parts of the world, and to observe their individual methods. It is fascinating that although Western palmistry developed independently from Indian and oriental palmistry all three systems agree on the basic meanings. I have also worked as a professional palmist in several countries, and given many hundreds of talks and lectures on the subject. I am still as enthusiastic about palmistry as I was at the age of ten, and hope some of that enthusiasm will rub off on to you as you read.

Palmistry began in Stone Age times. Pictures of human hands are frequently found in cave drawings, indicating their special interest in this part of the body. These paintings can be seen in the Lascaux Caves in France and the remarkable Santander Province Caves in Spain. In the innermost caves can be found walls covered with paintings of human hands. Similar pictures can be found in caves in Africa. It is fascinating to speculate on the purpose of these paintings.

According to Katharine St. Hill, author of *The Book of the Hand*, "the oldest manuscript that the world knows of, found among the venerable papyri of Egypt, is a prescription for the composition of women's face-paint, or 'make-up', and the second is a treatise on hand reading."

The ancient Vedic scriptures apparently contained much information on palmistry, and these were thousands of years old. K. C. Sen, an eminent Indian palmist, claims the earliest writings on palmistry were ancient Sanskrit verses which have been preserved and are still guarded from the public eye. Cheiro, a famous palmist at the turn of the century, claimed to have seen one of these manuscripts.

The ancient Greeks were keen traders and palmistry probably spread there from India. Aristotle wrote on the subject in *De Historia Animalium* some 2,500 years ago. Alexander the Great showed a great interest in every form of fortunetelling, including palmistry, and it is said that Aristotle wrote a book on the subject for him.

Palmistry is also mentioned favorably in the Old Testament:

".. . and he said, Wherefore doth my lord thus pursue after his servant? for what have I done? or what evil is in my hand?" (1 Samuel 26:18).

"He sealeth up the hand of every man, that all men may know his work" (Job 37:7).

"Length of days is in her right hand; and in her left hand riches and honor" (Proverbs 3:16).

"Behold, I have graven thee on the palms of my hands; thy walls are continually before me" (Isaiah 49:16).

Before the birth of Buddha in 563 B.C. the leading seers of the time gathered at the royal palace drawn by the extraordinary indications revealed in the stars. They were ecstatic to find the mark of the wheel in Buddha's hands and feet, indicating his future greatness. Palmists in India today still look for this special mark in the palms of babies.

In the eleventh century, Avicenna, an Arab physician, wrote his famous Canon of Medicine, which included material on the meanings of the shape and composition of the hand. This book was translated into Latin a century later and was largely responsible for the great interest in palmistry in Europe during the twelfth and thirteenth centuries. From that time on the number of books on palmistry increased rapidly. Unfortunately, just fragments remain of most of these. The *Digby Roll* in the Bodleian Library, dating from the early fifteenth century, is one of the oldest complete manuscripts on the subject. Not long after this the invention of printing started a flood of books on palmistry. The first of these was *Die Kunst Ciromantia* by Johann Hartlieb.

Gypsies come into the picture around this time, though doubtless they had been practicing palmistry for centuries before Sigismund, the Holy Roman Emperor, enlisted their aid as spies. Word of this soon spread and when Gypsies arrived at the gates of Paris in 1427 they were not allowed inside. However, the citizens of the city, intrigued and excited by these romantic strangers, rushed outside to have their fortunes told.

The tradition of crossing a Gypsy's palm with silver dates from this time. The Church claimed the Gypsies were in league with the Devil. To counter this the Gypsies explained that the Devil was afraid of both silver and the sign of the cross. Therefore, if you made a sign of the cross over a Gypsy's hand with silver you would be protected. Needless to say, the silver was retained by the Gypsies.

John Indagine, a Carthusian prior, helped popularize palmistry in Germany in the sixteenth century. His book, *Chiromantia*, was one of the first to be written in a popular style with stories of the author's experiences. A hundred years later the works of Dr. John Rothman, a German physician, became very popular and were translated into several languages. In England, Richard Saunders wrote a number of successful books full of dire predictions: "A Special line like a Globe on the backside of the thumb near the upward joynt, implies submersion viz., drowning in deep waters."

Two hundred years later the two most influential figures in the history of palmistry were born in France. The first of these was Stanislas D'Arpentigny. When he retired from the army he lived close to a wealthy landowner who was extremely interested in science. His wife was equally as absorbed in the arts. The landowner and his wife held weekly parties on different days for their friends. D'Arpentigny, interested in both the arts and science, was regularly invited to both parties. He was fascinated to discover that the landowner's scientific friends had fingers with knotted joints, whilst the wife's artistic friends possessed smooth fingers. He began studying the subject seriously and published his famous book, *La Cheirognomy*, in 1843. D'Arpentigny was not interested in the lines on the hand, concerning himself with the shape and texture of the hand and the length of fingers.

At the same time a portrait painter, Adolphe Desbarolles, was learning the Cabala with Eliphas Levi, the famous French occultist. Levi suggested that Desbarolles look at palmistry to see if he could bring it up to date. Desbarolles read everything he could find and soon began reading palms professionally. Unlike D'Arpentigny, Desbarolles was especially interested in the lines, and had no patience with people who claimed the lines on the palm were created by the opening and closing of the hand. "If anyone should tell you that these lines and signs in the palm have been traced by the movement of the hand, by its opening and closing, etc., answer them that these markings are found ten times more distinct and numerous in the hands of idle society women than in the palms of busy workers, and are also perfectly plain and strongly eloquent in the hands of babes but a few hours old." Desbarolles' aim was to update the traditions of "a science as old as the world." He did this admirably in his book *Les Mysteres de la Main*, which was published in 1860.

The next major development in palmistry was in the United States when William G. Benham published his monumental *The Laws of Scientific Hand Reading* in 1900. He synthesized the work of both D'Arpentigny and Desbarolles and taught that interpretations could be made only after an examination of both the shape and the lines on the hand. William Benham used a logical approach and believed that people with no intuition could still make excellent palm readers.

Interest in using palmistry for psychological analysis is a product of the twentieth century. The first major work on this subject was Julius Spier's *The Hands of Children*, which appeared in 1944 with an introduction by Carl Jung. This was quickly followed by works by Noel Jaquin, Charlotte Wolff, and—in the last ten years—Andrew Fizherbert.

Since World War II, research on palm patterns has been going on at the Kennedy-Galton Centre near London, and scientists are now beginning to confirm that health factors can be determined in the hand. The current research into dermatoglyphics (the study of skin patterns) has the potential to be the most exciting development yet in the history of palmistry. Although palmistry dates from Stone Age times, its greatest period is just beginning. The future of palmistry is assured now that scientists are proving its validity.

CHAPTER ONE

The Shape of the Hand

PALMS COME IN two categories: square and oblong. When looking at a hand, mentally remove the fingers and thumb and see if the palm is square or oblong in shape. This is your first clue about the person's character. Look at both hands. If your volunteer is right-handed this is the hand of everyday life, while the left hand indicates the person's imagination and inherited capabilities. A left-handed person's left hand is the hand of everyday life, and the right represents the imagination.

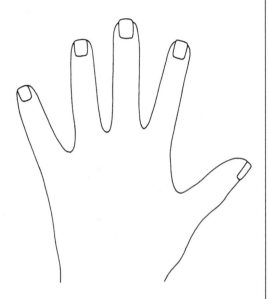

1a. Square-shaped hand

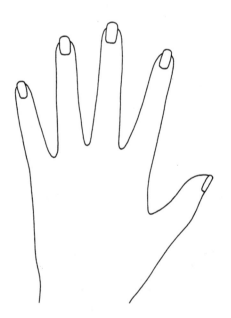

1b. Oblong-shaped hand

Square Hand

If the hand is square shaped (1a), we might say:

"You are a down-to-earth, capable, practical person. You have a great deal of energy and stamina and need to be kept busy. You keep your feet on the ground and like to see tangible evidence of something, rather than leaping to conclusions. You are a good worker, able to work hard and long when necessary."

Oblong Hand

If the hand is oblong shaped (1b), we might say this:

"You are inclined to be a bit of a dreamer at times. You have an imaginative approach to everything you do, and it is important that your work has a good deal of variety attached to it. Otherwise you are inclined to float away and live in your imagination. You come up with brilliant ideas, but getting started is sometimes difficult."

Naturally, you are going to see hands where you are not sure if they are really square or perhaps a little bit oblong. It is not possible to divide all of humanity into two distinct groups in this way, and consequently many people will have hands that do not conveniently fit into these two classifications. You may find someone with a square-shaped hand that has a decided bulge on the little finger side. This is still a square-shaped hand for our purposes, and we will cover the meaning of the bulge later on.

You may have read other classification systems in the past. The classic system divides hands into elementary (or primitive), practical, psychic, philosophic, and conic. This system was fine when it was first introduced in the late eighteenth century by a famous French palmist called D'Arpentigny, as people were classified more easily. A peasant, for instance, would have an elementary hand, while a wealthy nobleman might have a beautifully shaped conic hand. Nowadays, few people work in the fields and our hands have changed to reflect this, making the old system almost obsolete. I was taught this system as a child and still sometimes classify a palm as conic or philosophical, for instance, if it is very true to type. Usually though, I simply look for square or oblong.

It may be helpful to include brief descriptions of D'Arpentigny's hands as every now and again you will find someone with hands that fit perfectly into his system.

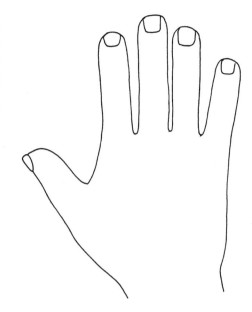

1c. Elementary hand

Elementary Hand

The elementary hand (1c) has a somewhat crude appearance. It is square in shape with short, stubby, rather shapeless fingers. The skin will be coarse and possibly hairy. There will be few lines on the palm, in some cases only three. People with elementary hands have few interests and can be very stubborn. They find it hard to express themselves in words, so can occasionally become violent when frustrated. As long as their basic needs are being met they take life exactly as it comes, sparing no thought for tomorrow.

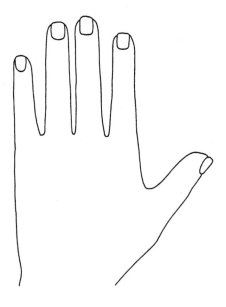

1d. Practical hand

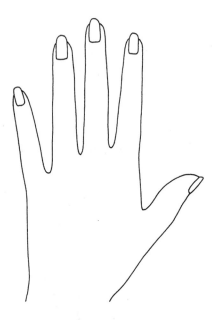

1e. Conic hand

Practical Hand

Next up from the elementary hand is the practical hand (1d). This also has a square-shaped palm, but with longer, better shaped fingers than the elementary hand. The skin is less coarse and there are more lines on the palm. People with practical hands have a variety of interests and can turn their hands to almost anything—hence the name "practical."

Conic Hand

The conic hand (1e) has a graceful, curved appearance. The palm is more oblong than square, and the fingers are usually fairly long with rounded tips. The palm will feel fleshy. People with conic palms are creative, aesthetic, and often day-dreamers. They visualize a beautiful world where everything is perfect. They dislike vulgar language or cruelty of any sort.

Psychic Hand

This is the shape that artists love. The hand and fingers are long, slender, and graceful. People with this type of hand are idealistic, intuitive, and impractical. They spend much of their time in a fantasy world rather than facing the realities of life. Psychic hands (1f) are found frequently in India and the Far East, but seldom in the West.

Philosophical Hand

The philosophical hand (1g) is usually square in shape. The long fingers have very obvious joints. These people like to analyze everything. You can use an analogy of thoughts coming in from the tips of the fingers, reaching the first joint and having to go around and around before moving on to the second joint where the process is repeated. As a result, the thought is well analyzed by the time it reaches the palm.

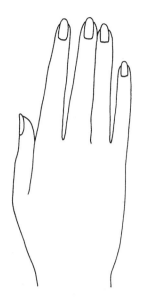

1f. Psychic hand

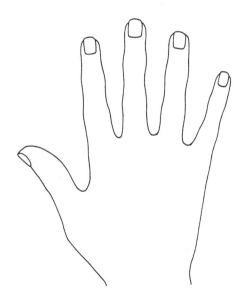

1g. Philosophical hand

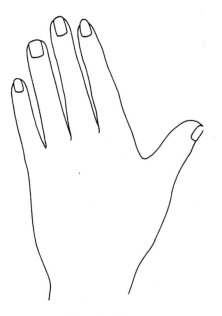

1h. Mixed hand

Mixed Hand

You will find many people fit perfectly into D'Arpentigny's system. He classified everyone who did not as having mixed hands (1h). Fortunately, the system we have begun with the square-and oblong-shaped palms can conveniently classify everyone. The shape of the palm is only half of the system, though. To complete the classification we need to move on to the fingers.

CHAPTER TWO

Hand and Finger Combinations

AFTER DETERMINING IF the palm is square or oblong, we look at the fingers to see if they are short or long. This is not easy to gauge when you are just beginning, but a little practice will enable you to assess the finger length at a glance.

The fingers are usually long if they can fold back and touch a spot at least seven-eighths of the way along the palm. Unfortunately, there are exceptions as some people have extremely flexible hands whilst others are very stiff. Also, someone with an extremely oblong palm may have long fingers that reach only halfway

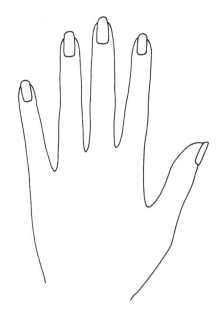

2a. Long fingers

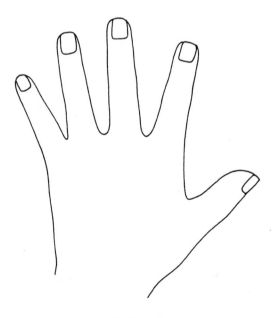

2b. Short fingers

along as the palm itself is very long. With experience you will be able to look at someone's palm and instantly know if the fingers are long or short. The problem comes when you are first learning and find a hand with fingers that seem to be neither long nor short. Fortunately, we can cover that situation as well.

Long Fingers

If the fingers are long (2a) the person pays attention to detail and we can say:

> "You enjoy work that has a lot to it. You are patient and enjoy all the fiddly bits—you like the details of things. Whatever work you do has to be very involving. If it is too simple you would lose interest very quickly."

Short Fingers

Someone with short fingers (2b) is almost the opposite. He will be more interested in the broad strokes rather than the details and will not have much patience. We could say to this person:

> "You are always busy. Sometimes you may start something new before you've finished the last task. There can often be several things on the go all at the same time. You tend to want everything right now, so patience is not your

strong suit. Your impulsiveness is bound to have got you into trouble at times in the past. In some ways you are a jack-of-all-trades."

Medium-Length Fingers

Naturally, someone with fingers that are neither long nor short will fall into a middle category (2c). We might say:

"At times you can be very patient. At other times, however, you are inclined to jump first and think afterwards. If something really interests you, you want to get right down to the bottom of it and work it all out. If it is only a passing interest, you are more inclined to skim over the surface and not learn it in much detail."

We now have four possibilities to look at: square hands with short fingers, square hands with long fingers, oblong hands with short fingers, and oblong hands with long fingers. This is the classification system used in Chinese palmistry. I first learned of it in Fred Gettings' monumental book, *The Book of the Hand*. The four types are named after the four elements of the ancients: fire, earth, air, and water. These relate very well to the descriptions of the fire, earth, air, and water signs of astrology, but it does not necessarily follow that a Sagittarian (a fire sign), for instance, would have a fire hand. You can find people with all four types of hand in every sign of the zodiac.

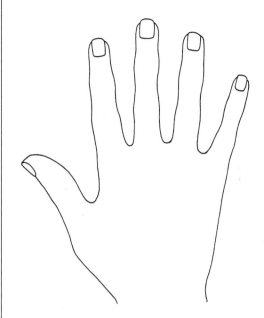

2c. Medium-length fingers

Fire Hands

Fire is hot, energizing, and constantly moving. It can provide gentle heat, but can also burn. Consequently, it needs careful handling. A fire hand is oblong with short fingers (2d). Someone with a hand like this is likely to be emotional, enthusiastic, and creative. The short fingers give a dislike for detail, and the long palm adds intuition. For someone with a hand like this we might say:

"You have a great mind, full of wonderful ideas that you get very excited about. These enthusiasms may not last for long, but they are extremely important to you at the time. Your emotions can be a bit hard to handle on occasion, but they do enable you to experience

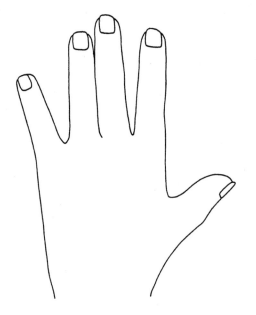

2d. Fire hands

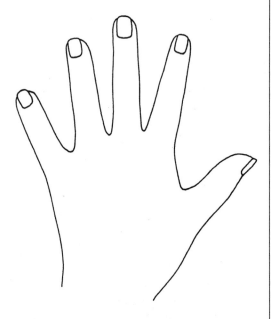

2e. Earth hands

everything to the fullest, making the most of what life has to offer. Details are not your strong point, and you tend to prefer the overall picture to the fiddly bits. You are likely to be creative in some sort of way, and need to be busy to be happy."

Earth Hands

Earth is the dry, solid part of our planet. Everything that happens on Earth is subject to the natural rhythms of germination, growth, death, and decay. Earth is timeless, and expresses stability. Below its surface, however, all sorts of changes are constantly occurring. This can lead to earthquakes and other upheavals. The earth hand is much like the practical hand. It consists of a square palm and short fingers (2e). People with this type of hand are reliable, down-to-earth, and practical. They enjoy repetitive work and are good with their hands. They enjoy rhythm. They are conservative, reserved, and possessive. However, like Earth itself, they can also react violently if they deem it necessary. We might say to someone with earth hands:

"You are a good hard worker. You enjoy physical challenges, and your hands can think for themselves. You can be stubborn at times, and it would be impossible to move you once your mind is made up. You enjoy rhythm and movement. You are not usually good with the details, unless you are making something. You probably prefer working out of doors, doing something practical. You are reliable, honest, and somewhat reserved."

Air Hands

Air is essential for life. We take it for granted and seldom notice it except on windy days. Air is also essential for communication, as it carries sound waves. Creatures of the air, such as birds and flying insects, are fast moving and active. The air hand consists of a square palm and long fingers (2f). These people tend to use logic more than their intuition. They are quick-witted and express themselves clearly. They enjoy communicating, and often make careers in these fields. The strong emphasis on logic means that these people tend to distrust emotions—both their own and other people's. We could say something along these lines to someone with air hands:

"You are intelligent, clear-thinking, and discriminating. Relationships are important to you, but you sometimes find logic getting in the way of your feelings. You are reliable and like to do things properly. You have a quick, analytical brain and can express yourself very well when you choose. You are a stimulating companion and life is never dull when you are around."

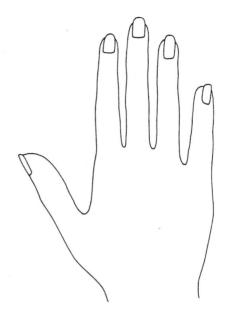

2f. Air hands

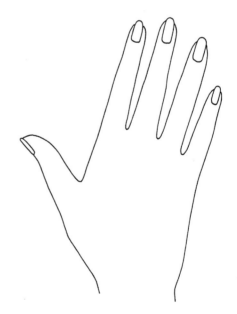

2g. Water hands

Water Hands

Finally, water. If you think about it, water is essentially still. Other forces have to act upon it to make it change. It is also shapeless—it simply moves to fill up whatever shape is available. The Moon has a strong influence on water, creating the tides in our oceans. The saying, "Still waters run deep," is very pertinent to the water hand. The water hand consists of an oblong palm with long fingers (2g). It is sometimes called the intuitive hand, as these people are extremely aware and receptive. People with this type of hand are changeable, impressionable, and emotional. They are idealistic and highly imaginative. You could say to someone with water hands:

"You have an extremely rich inner life. Your imagination is keen and you fantasize about just about everything. You can be influenced by others, so you can be changeable in your ideas. Your intuition is strong. You are emotional. If you are keen on someone, you love spending time in their company, but you also need time by yourself to reflect on matters going on in your own life. You are happiest inside the right relationship with someone to depend and rely upon."

CHAPTER THREE

More Observations on the Hand

MOST PEOPLE THINK palmistry is simply a matter of reading the lines on the hands. You already know that is not the case. Before we move on to examine the lines, let's have a quick look at the hand generally. We now know if the person has a fire, earth, air, or water hand, which immediately gives us a great deal of information. With just a quick scan of the hand we can increase our knowledge enormously.

Fleshy and Padded Palms

First, look to see if the hand is fleshy or well padded. It may almost seem spongy to the touch in extreme cases. If the hand is fleshy the person will desire a lot of the luxuries of life, and is likely to readily indulge in the pleasures of such activities. If the hand is the opposite, and feels hard to the touch, you will have found someone who is more stoic and better able to withstand the ups and downs of life. He or she will be able to stay away from different pleasures if other things are more important at the time.

Coarse or Refined

Next, look to see if the hand is coarse or refined in appearance. Do not be fooled by the calluses created by hard physical labor. It is perfectly possible for a manual laborer to have refined hands. A coarse hand is one in which the pores in the skin are very obvious. This is often easier to see on the back of the hand.

People with very coarse hands have largely animal instincts and appetites. They have a limited range of needs and will be perfectly happy as long as these are being met. They will be likely to overindulge when the opportunity presents itself. They will also be "thick-skinned."

People with refined hands are more cultured and aesthetic in every way. They are likely to be interested in different forms of creativity, and will certainly want their home and work environments to be as attractive as possible.

Hair

While looking at the back of the hand, you can also see the amount of hair present. A small amount of hair indicates masculinity and is desirable on a man's hand. A large amount of hair denotes someone with large physical appetites that have to be met for the person to be happy.

How the Hand Is Held

While the person is holding their hands out to you for a reading, look to see if the fingers are held together or apart. People who hold their fingers together (3a) are likely to be introspective, wary, and often lacking in confidence. People who display their hands with the fingers spread apart (3b) are far more confident and outgoing. They will be much more self-assured than the people who hold their fingers together.

Some people start out by holding their hands straight, but gradually close their hands before your gaze. These people will always have their fingers held together, and the closing action indicates a fear that you will discover their innermost secrets.

The Four Quadrants

The hand is divided into four sections by two imaginary lines (3c). The first one runs down the Saturn (second) finger and on to the wrist. This divides the palm into outer- and inner-directed areas. The outer area is the half that includes the thumb, and this relates to our actions in the world. The other half relates to our inner-directed thoughts and actions.

The second imaginary line starts under the thumb, halfway between the base of the fingers and the start of the wrist. It is a horizontal line running across the palm. The half that includes the fingers relates to activity, whilst the remaining half is more passive, or receptive.

These two lines divide the hand into four quadrants: the active-outer, active-inner, passive-outer, and passive-inner. When you look at the hand, check to see if one of these divisions is more prominent than the others. This is a subjective thing, really. One quadrant may appear more prominent because of the different mounts (little bumps) inside it, or you may just get an impression that one area is more important than the others. It always pays to follow your intuitive feelings when reading palms. If no one section appears more dominant than the others, the person will have managed to balance the different areas of life.

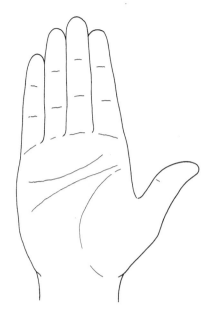

3a. Closed hand

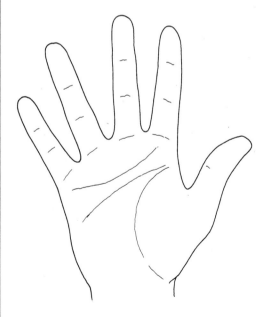

3b. Open hand

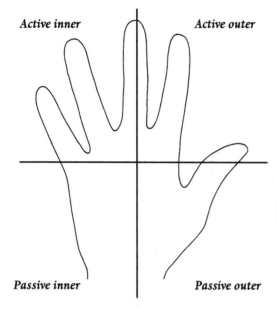

Active inner   *Active outer*

Passive inner   *Passive outer*

3c. The four quadrants

Active-outer Quadrant

The active-outer quadrant includes the top section of the thumb, plus the first finger and half of the second finger. This area deals with the person's ambitions and goals. If this area is dominant, the person will put a great deal of thought and effort into achieving success.

Passive-outer Quadrant

Immediately below this is the passive-outer quadrant, which includes the bottom half of the thumb, plus the mound below it (mount of Venus). This quadrant deals with physical stamina and sexuality. If this area is well-developed, the person will possess a great deal of physical energy and stamina, and have a strong sexual appetite. If this area appears to be the weakest of the four quadrants, the person will not be as concerned with physical activities, and would find it difficult to generate much enthusiasm for anything.

Active-inner Quadrant

The active-inner quadrant includes the ring and little fingers as well as half of the second finger. If this quadrant is dominant, the person will have more interest in learning and the arts than in achieving great worldly success.

Passive-inner Quadrant

Finally we come to the passive-inner quadrant. This encompasses an area we will discuss later called the mount of Luna. This area deals with the creative subconscious, and if this area is dominant the person will be very aware of his or her feelings, subtle nuances, and intuition. It also relates to the imagination and is likely to be well developed in the hands of people engaged in creative pursuits, such as artists, poets, and musicians.

CHAPTER FOUR

Lines on
the Hand

AT LAST WE COME to the part that most people recognize as being "palmistry"—the reading of the lines on the palm (4a).

You will quickly discover that no two palms are alike, and even the right and left palms of the same person are different. Some people have very few lines on their palms, whilst other people possess a network of hundreds and hundreds of fine lines.

Most lines are caused by worry. Consequently, someone with just three lines on his or her palm is likely to have an easier life than someone with hundreds. However, taken to the

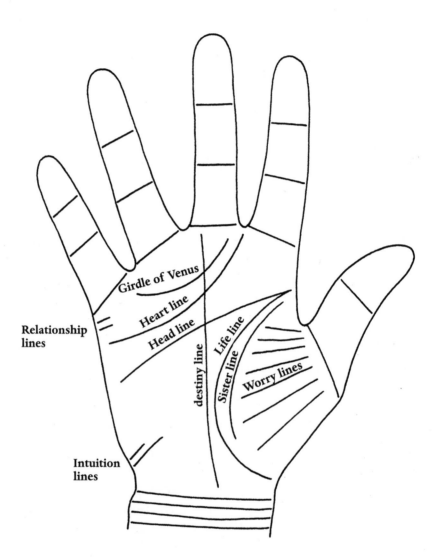

Relationship
lines

Girdle of Venus

Heart line

Head line

destiny line

Life line

Sister line

Worry lines

Intuition
lines

4a. The main lines

extreme of just three lines, this person's life is likely to be very dull and uninteresting. As with everything in palmistry, a balance is required, so we look for a hand with a reasonable number of clearly defined lines.

Defects on the Lines

The quality of the lines shows the vitality of the particular aspect of the person's life governed by each particular line. Ideally, the lines should be clearly visible, reasonably deep, and without any defects on them. There are a number of possible defects. A dot or small spot is often found on a line. This is an obstacle that temporarily impedes progress. A series of dots indicates a recurring problem.

4b. Squares and grilles

Squares

Squares (4b) are positive in nature, and represent protection. They often surround breaks in a line, and this is a sign that the person is protected and will ultimately triumph over whatever the difficulty may be.

4c. Islands

Grilles

A grille is always a negative indication. It shows that the person does not see the situation as clearly as he or she would like and consequently wastes time and energy. This can be extremely frustrating.

Crosses

A cross on a line represents changes. This can be good or bad. The cross needs to be distinct and not created by another line overlapping the first.

Islands

Islands (4c) are the little bubbles or ovals inside a line, and they reveal scattered energy. They relate to uncertainty, frustration, and emotional difficulties. You will often find a number of islands together forming a braiding effect.

Triangles

A triangle is found comparatively rarely and relates to the intellect. It shows the person is shrewd and quick-thinking.

It pays to have a set way of reading a palm to ensure that nothing is missed. After assessing the shape and quality of the palm and the fingers, I move on to the major lines which are read in this order: heart line, head line, life line, and destiny line.

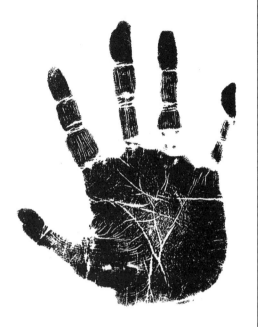

4d. Few lines, left hand

4f. Many lines, left hand

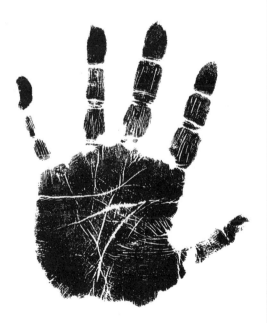

4e. Few lines, right hand

4g. Many lines, right hand

CHAPTER FIVE

The Heart Line

THE HEART LINE governs our emotional lives and shows how we relate to others. It is the major line nearest the fingers, running across the palm from the side of the hand under the little finger and usually ending in the area between the first and second fingers.

There are two main types of heart line: the physical heart line and the mental heart line.

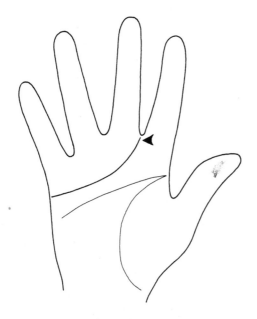

5a. Physical heart line

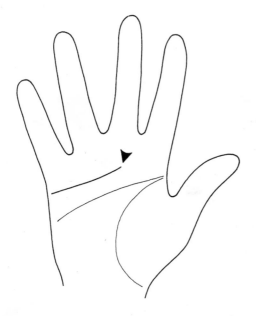

5b. Mental heart line

Physical Heart Line

The physical heart line (5a) curves towards the end and finishes either on or between the first two fingers. People with physical heart lines are generally able to express their feelings well. Although they suffer their share of ups and downs, they pick themselves up quickly and get on with their lives. They are likely to express their feelings in a physical, assertive manner. We could say to someone with this type of heart line:

"As your heart line ends right up under the fingers, it shows that you have an open nature and can express your innermost feelings. You are warm and affectionate. When things go wrong you manage to pick yourself up quickly."

Mental Heart Line

A mental heart line (5b) comes right across the palm and does not curve at the end. People with mental heart lines find it hard to express their innermost feelings. They will suffer in silence rather than make a scene. They will have plenty of romantic feelings, which take precedence over common sense. They are sensitive and need plenty of space around them. We might say:

"You have a heart line that comes right across your palm. This is known as a mental heart line, and it makes it rather difficult for you to express your innermost feelings. If you work at this it will gradually become easier for you. You can be rather sensitive at times and possibly bottle things up a bit. You like people, but definitely need a bit of room around you at the same time."

As the heart line governs the emotions it is unusual to find one without defects, as all of us have ups and downs at different times in our lives. The most usual visible sign of this is a series of islands on the heart line at the time these difficulties occurred (5c). These problems are generally relationship ones, and consequently it is very easy to determine if, for instance, someone had an unhappy marriage followed by a happy one. In this case, the earlier part of the person's life (the part nearest the little finger) will have a multitude of islands, whilst the rest of the line will be clear.

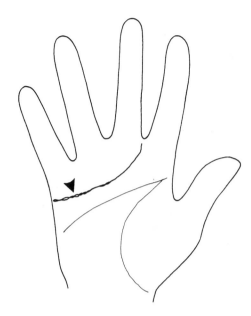

5c. Heart line with islands

Ending Positions

Where the heart line finishes is extremely important. Ideally, it should end between the first and second fingers (5d) as this gives a balance between the ego (represented by the first finger) and the rest of humanity. People with this are realistic about their emotional life, and do not have impossible expectations.

If the line ends on or directly under the first finger (5e), the person will be idealistic and

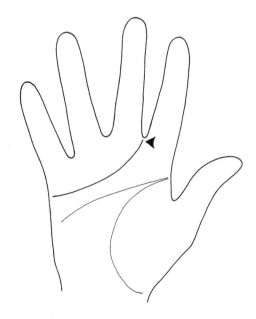

5d. Heart line ending between Jupiter and Saturn fingers

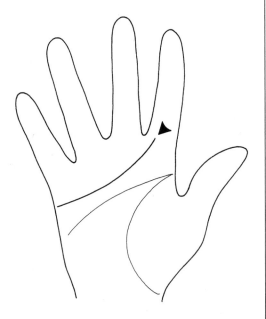

5e. Heart line ending under Jupiter finger

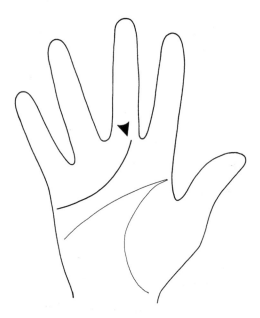

5f. Heart line ending under Saturn finger

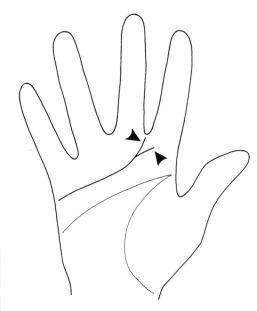

5g. Forked heart line

easily hurt. Other people will seldom live up to their expectations, leading to frequent disappointments.

If the heart line ends on or directly under the second finger (5f), the person is inclined to be selfish and think only of his or her own gratification. There will be a lack of emotional involvement.

Often you will find a heart line that forks in two directions (5g) at the end. This makes for someone who has a complex emotional nature. He or she will also be able to see both sides of a situation.

If the heart line ends with three or more branches (5h), it is an indication of someone who is extremely emotional in all romantic relationships. It is often regarded as being a

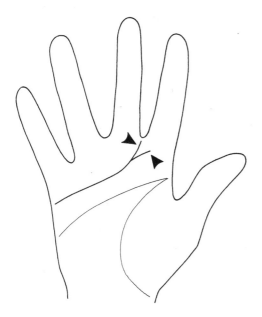

5h. Heart line with many branches

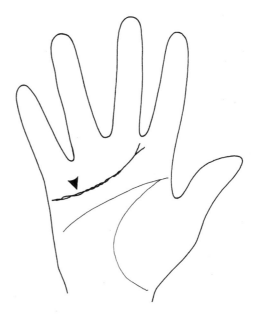

5i. Chained heart line

"lucky" sign, but this is true only if the person is inside a strong, stable, mutually supportive relationship.

Special Marks

The quality of the heart line provides information about the person's enjoyment of life. Ideally, it should be well marked, deep, and clear. This is an indication of a happy emotional life and a strong heart.

Chains (5i) on the heart line reveal emotional tension—many ups and downs. Crosses and breaks are a sign of emotional loss—the end of a relationship, possibly through death. An island shows a period of depression.

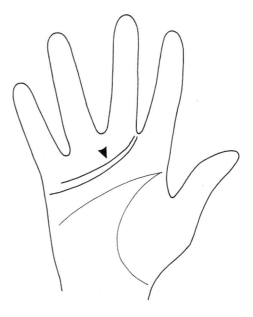

5j. Doubled heart line

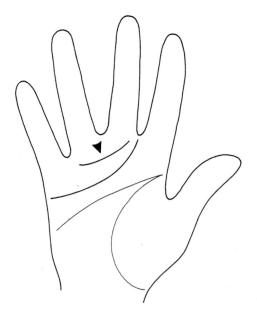

5k. Girdle of Venus

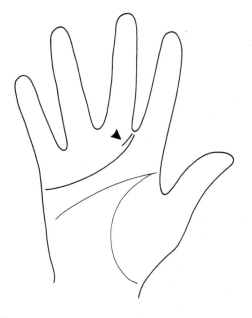

5l. Lasting relationship

If the heart line is doubled (5j), it is a sign that the person's lover will be extremely caring and protective.

For compatibility purposes it is best if the two people have heart lines that end in the same part of the palm. We will discuss compatibility later.

The Girdle of Venus

Very often, you will find a fine line between the heart line and the base of the fingers. This is called the girdle of Venus (5k) and denotes extreme sensitivity. It is found most frequently in water hands. People with a girdle of Venus need constant stimulation and variety. This can often be channeled into some form of creativity. A girdle of Venus that is made up of a number of lines parallel to each other creates an extremely sensitive, highly emotional person who may be unstable and neurotic.

Long Lasting Relationship

Frequently, there is a fine line parallel to the heart line at the very end (5l). This denotes that the person will have a long-lasting relationship that is still there in his or her old age.

CHAPTER SIX

The Head Line

THE HEAD LINE governs the person's intellect and shows the quality of his or her thinking at different stages of life. It also reveals how the person will approach problems, and reveals much about his or her attitude toward life.

It is said that the longer the line is, the more intelligent the person will be. The presence of a long head line, however, does not necessarily mean that the person will use that ability. After all, none of us use more than a mere fraction of our mental potential. We could learn a new fact every second of our lives from the moment of

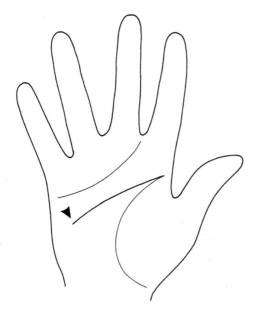

6a. Imaginative head line

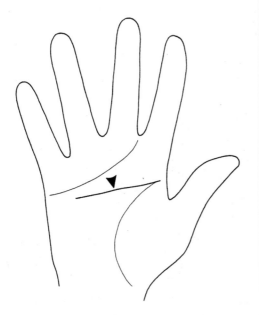

6b. Practical head line

birth and not run out of brain capacity. Consequently, most of us are making use of just a few percent of our potential. Someone with a short head line who uses it will invariably do much better in life than a lazy thinker with a long line. It is better to use the length of the head line to estimate how detailed a person's thinking is. The longer the line, the more complex and involved the thinking.

The head line begins between the base of the thumb and the first finger and goes part of the way across the palm. In a few instances it can completely cross the palm. It should be clear and well defined. Ideally, it will not have any negative marks on it. For instance, any islands or chains on this line indicate a time when the person was thinking in a muddled sort of way and had an inability to concentrate.

The degree of slope of the line indicates the amount of imagination the person has. If the line runs straight across the palm, the person will be practical, but unimaginative. If it slopes down toward the wrist the person will be imaginative, and this quality increases with the degree of slope. Obviously, it can sometimes slope so far down that the person can be out of touch with reality. You will find these deeply sloping head lines most frequently in water hands.

As with the heart line, we can divide the head line into two main types: the imaginative head line and the practical head line.

The Imaginative Head Line

The imaginative head line (6a) has a decided curve on it and heads toward the wrist. It ends in the part of the hand called the creative sub-conscious, giving the person creativity and a good imagination. We might say to someone with this type of head line:

"You have a creative, imaginative approach to everything you do. It is important that whatever work you do is absorbing to you, as otherwise you would quickly float away into your imagination. You work best in aesthetic surroundings, and appreciate nice things around you. You have refined tastes."

The Practical Head Line

The other main type of head line is the practical one (6b). This line runs straight across the palm. As the name suggests, this belongs to people who have their feet firmly on the ground and live very much in the present. We could say:

"You have a practical, down-to-earth approach to everything you do. You do not take too much on trust, preferring to work things out for yourself. You like to get down to the bottom of things and make up your own mind."

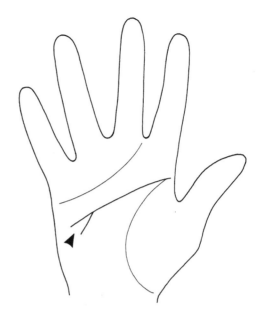

6c. Writer's fork

I have two good friends who make their living as writers. One writes popular romance novels and the other is a magazine journalist. As you might expect, the romance writer has an imaginative head line, whilst the journalist has a practical head line. They are both well suited for their respective careers.

The Writer's Fork

Every now and again you will find a forked head line (6c). One branch goes up to the creative subconscious whilst the other goes straight across the palm. This combination is known as the writer's fork. It means that the person has a vivid imagination, and can come

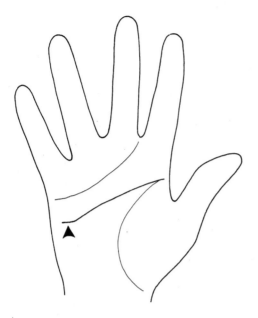

6d. Material needs shown on head line

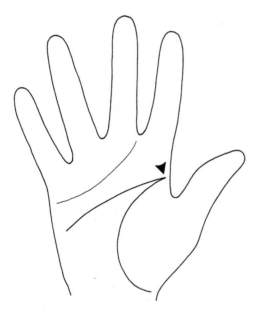

6e. Head line joined to life line at start

up with good ideas which he or she can then make real. Writers do this, of course, but so do all sorts of other people. It would be a definite asset to a business person, for instance, just as it would be for a creative artist. One of my teachers at school had a wonderful gift of creating exciting similes that made learning much easier for the class. He had a very well-defined writer's fork on his hand.

Material Needs

A head line that turns up at the end toward the fingers indicates someone with strong material needs (6d). A young girl determined to find a wealthy husband would be bound to have this line, as would a business person who was obsessed with becoming a millionaire. In some instances, the presence of this line can be an asset, but usually it describes someone who is driven and does not know when to stop.

Starting Positions

If the head line touches the life line at the start (6e), it means the person is cautious and thinks first. If the head line is separated, but still close to the life line (6f), it is an indication of a confident person who has been an independent thinker since birth. The further away the head line starts from the life line (6g), the more inde-

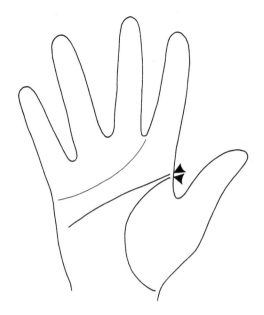

6f. Head line starting separately from life line

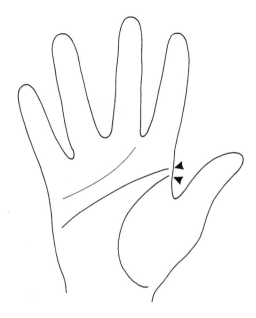

6g. Head line apart from life line at start

pendent the person will be. If it starts from the mount of Jupiter (the mound at the base of the first finger) (6h), it is an indication of someone who is extremely ambitious and will not allow anyone or anything to get in the way of his or her path to the top. If the head line starts inside the life line (6i), it is an indication of lack of confidence, probably due to family reasons in the early years of life. If the head line starts attached to the life line (6j) and remains joined for some distance, it shows that the family influence was so strong that the person was not able (or was not willing) to make decisions on his or her own.

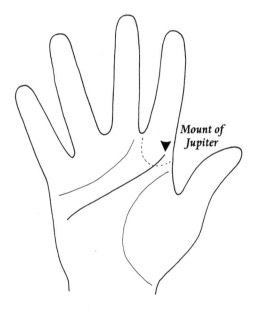

Mount of Jupiter

6h. Head line starting in mount of Jupiter

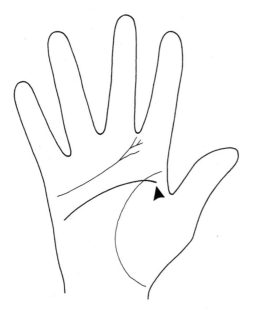

6i. Head line starting inside the life line

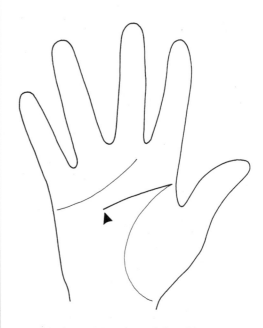

6k. Average-length head line

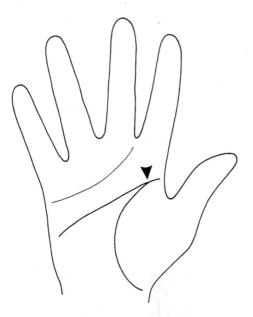

6j. Head line attached to life line at start

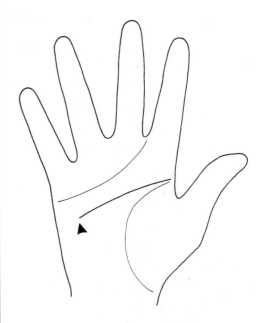

6l. Long head line

Length of the Head Line

An average length head line runs across the palm and ends somewhere under the ring finger (6k).

A long head line is an indication of a quick-thinking, versatile person with many interests (6l).

If the head line runs right across the palm to the opposite side (6m), it shows that the person has enormous powers of insight. In effect, this line divides the palm in two, affecting the energy flow.

People with short head lines (6n) are straightforward, practical thinkers. They want to get in and do the job without wasting too much time. They do not analyze things to the degree their long head-lined friends will.

Marks on the Head Line

Ideally, the head line is long, clear, and well-marked, showing intelligence and good, logical thinking.

If the line has an island on it, it shows a time when the person's thinking was confused, possibly caused by problems arising between what the person would like to do and what he or she actually has to do. It indicates a time of mental crisis. In extreme cases, this can indicate a nervous breakdown.

Chains on the line are a sign of stress and tension, and a time when the brain was not

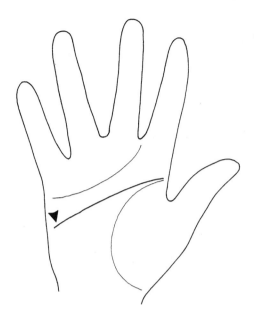

6m. Very long head line

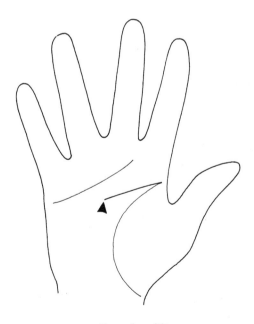

6n. Short head line

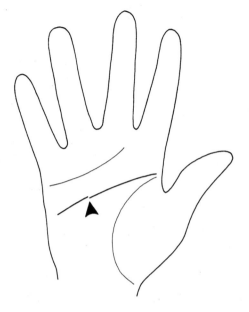

60. Break in the head line

being used as it should. This could be caused by depression. It can also often be an indicator of severe headaches. Small, perpendicular lines crossing the head line can also indicate headaches.

A break in the head line (60) shows a time when the brain was not being used. This is usually because the person was unconscious for a period, or perhaps was suffering from a head injury.

If the head line is faint and thin in appearance, the person will not be putting any energy into his or her thought processes and will be a lazy thinker. If the line is also long it shows that the person will give the impression that he or she knows much more than he or she really does.

If the head line is faint and broad, it shows the person is a sluggish thinker who will take a long time to come up with ideas.

CHAPTER SEVEN

The Life Line

THIS IS THE ONE line that everyone knows! I couldn't begin to estimate the number of times people have come up to me and said, "My Johnny's got a very short life line. Does that mean he'll die young?" Many children have short life lines and this line lengthens as they grow.

It is impossible to tell when someone will die by looking at their life line. Several other factors are also involved. Moreover, it is inexcusable for any palmist to tell someone when they are going to die, as their prediction could

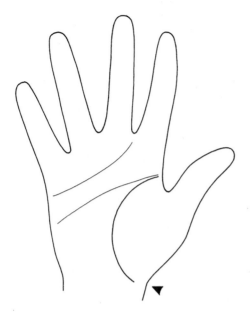

7a. The life line

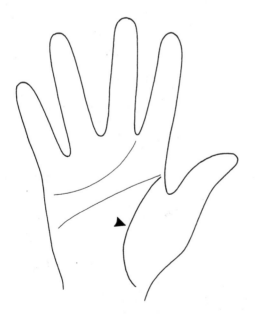

7b. Life line hugging the thumb

become a self-fulfilling prophecy. When my aunt was fifteen a palm reader told her she would die at the age of sixty-five. For years before she reached sixty-five she worried about the prediction and was not free of a sense of fear till she turned sixty-six. Fortunately, she did not die at the age she was told she would, but she experienced years of needless stress and anxiety despite many other psychics telling her the prediction was wrong. Why did the palmist tell her she would die at sixty-five? It is possible that her hand did indicate death at sixty-five when she was fifteen. But the palmist ignored the fact that our hands are constantly changing, so what she thought was definitely death at sixty-five was altered as my aunt's hands changed over the years. I never tell anyone when they are going to die, even if the date seems obvious to me, and I urge you to do the same. After all, the hands can change and nullify your prediction.

A short life line does not indicate a short life, just as a long line does not guarantee a long life. You will find some people with all three main lines (life, head, and heart) short.

The life line is the first line that is formed on the palm and appears by the time the human embryo is eight weeks old. This line is quickly followed by the heart line and then the head line. It is interesting to reflect that these lines appear long before the baby is able to make any movements, so can not be dismissed as being merely "flexure" lines caused by the bending of the hand as some critics of palmistry claim.

The life line is a measure of a person's vitality and interest in life. It is a picture of the person's life force and reflects the quality of life. It also shows how much strength and energy the person has at his or her disposal.

The life line is the line that encircles the thumb (7a), starting from the edge of the palm on the side of the first finger and going in a semicircle around the mound at the base of the thumb.

Like the other lines it should be clear and well marked. Ideally, it should come as far across the palm as possible, as the area encircled by this line (the mount of Venus) indicates the amount of energy and stamina the individual has. Someone with a life line that hugs the thumb (7b) will be listless, lethargic, and lacking in energy. Conversely, someone with a life line that comes well across the palm (7c) will have plenty of energy and will be more vibrant and enthusiastic about life.

We could say to someone with a life line that hugs the thumb:

> "At times you do not have quite the energy you would like to have. You need to make sure that you get enough rest and relaxation. Pay some attention to physical fitness and your stamina will increase."

This is in contrast to what we could say to someone with a life line that comes well out across the palm:

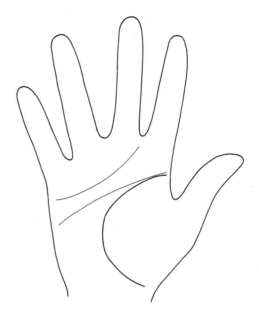

7c. Life line coming well across the palm

> "You have plenty of stamina and energy at your disposal. If you're doing something you enjoy, you could go on indefinitely. You enjoy doing physical activities, and when you get tired, you sleep it off very quickly and wake ready to start again."

The Sister Line

A lot of people have a fine line inside and parallel to the life line (7d). This is usually found near the start of the life line, but can appear anywhere. Some fortunate people have it all the way through their lives, giving the impression

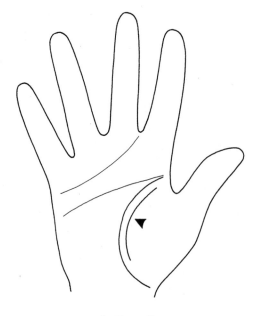

7d. Sister line

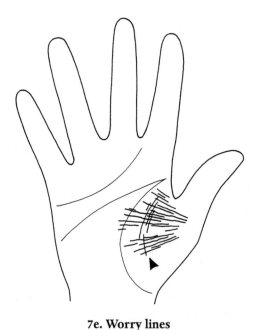

7e. Worry lines

of having two life lines. This line is called a sister line, as it is sister to the life line. It protects the individual at the time indicated by the life line. This means that something that could really hurt one person would not be felt as severely by someone with a sister line on their palm. I know a woman who survived a major bus accident in which almost everyone else died. She has a very strong sister line on her palm. This line is always a fortunate thing to find on a hand. If it is found near the end of the life line it indicates someone who will be physically active in his or her old age.

Worry Lines

The mound that is encompassed by the life line is called the mount of Venus and we will be covering it in more detail later on. A large number of people have fine lines radiating from the base of the thumb toward, and sometimes even crossing, the life line (7e). These fine lines are called worry lines. You can rest assured that you will find many hands with plenty of these! A person with what appears to be hundreds of these fine lines will be someone who worries about everything. If there are just a few lines, these will indicate the times when the person has something serious to worry about. You will also find some people with none of these lines. These people never worry about anything—but you can bet that their partner will have hundreds of lines! If the lines cross the life line it is an indication of serious worry that has or could affect the person's health. If this is in the person's future I will tell them about it, and try and encourage them to learn meditation or self-hypnosis to help them control worry.

Breaks in the Life Line

Breaks in the life line are usually not serious, contrary to popular belief. A break indicates a major change in the person's life at the time indicated (7f). This is usually a change in outlook, and the person is likely to alter the way he or she looks at things at the time indicated. Generally, the life line overlaps itself at these times, providing a sort of brief sister line to make the change as smooth as possible. Sometimes, though, the change can be fairly dramatic. It could be a relationship breakup or a health problem, for instance. It is often possible to determine exactly what the problem is by looking at other parts of the hand, and we will learn how to synthesize this information later.

Time on the Life Line

Timing is not easy on the hand, and a number of methods have been devised to do this. Probably the simplest way is to draw an imaginary line down the palm from the middle of the Saturn (second) finger. Where it reaches the life line is about the age of thirty-five (7g).

Another method is to measure the length of the life line. Where it reaches the base of the palm and turns to go around the thumb is regarded as being the age of seventy. Measure

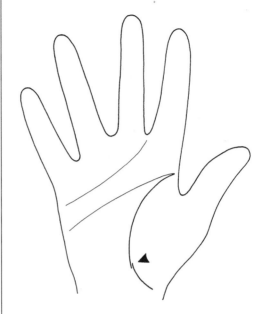

7f. Break on life line

the length of the line from where it begins to this point, and you can work out time fairly accurately. For instance, half of the length will give you the age of thirty-five. In India I have seen palmists using a very similar system to this using a length of thread to measure the line. Some people have life lines that go right around the thumb and finish only because the skin patterns end. This is regarded as marking out one hundred years. Remember though, that the presence of an extremely long life line does not necessarily indicate a long life. All we can do by measuring the life line is to record periods of time.

Another method is to divide the life line into three equal sections from where it begins to about the age of seventy. Each section indicates twenty to twenty-five years (7h).

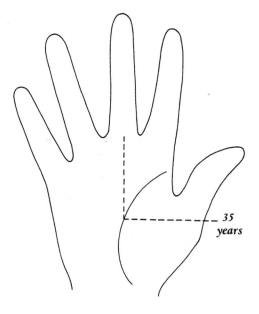

7g. Thirty-five-year method of timing.

I have found it very helpful to use the life line to determine important events from the person's past. This is usually an illness, accident, or time when the person felt in danger of death. By knowing when these events occurred I can then measure future time more accurately.

Cheiro had a system of dividing the life and destiny lines into seven-year periods (7i). In Germany, many palmists date events from the wrist up. This is due to the influence of Julius Spier, celebrated author of *The Hands of Children*. (He was responsible for Carl Jung's interest in palmistry.)

As you can see, it is difficult to date events accurately on a palm. Every measuring system has disadvantages and none is 100 percent accurate.

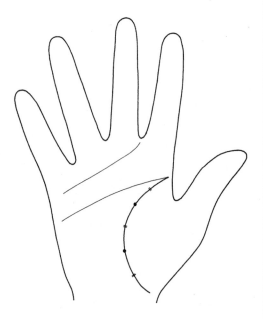

7h. Three-section method of timing.

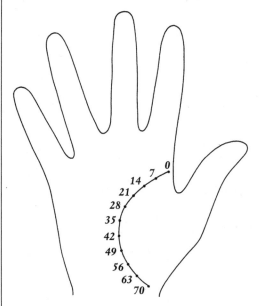

7i. Seven-year method of timing.

Marks on the Life Line

Like the other main lines, the life line should be well marked and clear. In practice few people have life lines like this.

A square on the life line can be positive in some situations, and the opposite in others. It is a positive sign when a square forms to enclose a break in the life line (7j). This is known as a protective square, and is an indication that the person will have enough energy and stamina to handle the situation. Squares that cover the life line, but are not enclosing breaks (7k), are an indication of confinement. This could mean life in a closed environment, such as a monastery. It is more likely to indicate prison. Twenty years ago I read the palm of a young man who had several of these squares on his palm. I explained what they meant. Fortunately, he took some note of my words and when I saw him again several months later the squares had disappeared. Because he had changed his way of life, his hand had changed to reflect the new person.

Islands on the life line are an indication of depression and possible hospitalization.

A chained life line is a sign of many health problems, usually of an emotional nature.

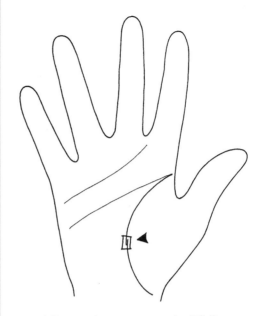

7j. Protective square on the life line

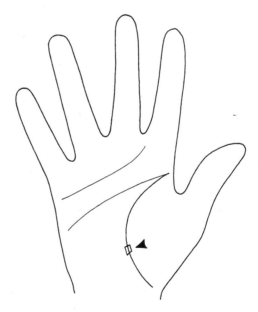

7k. Square on the lifeline

CHAPTER EIGHT

The Destiny Line

So FAR WE have covered lines that are found on everyone's hands. From now on we will be covering lines that not everyone has.

The destiny line is the line that runs down the hand somewhere near the middle of the palm, starting near the wrist and running towards the fingers. It is complicated in that it can start anywhere near the base of the palm. However, it usually starts somewhere in the middle of the palm, close to the wrist, and heads toward the Saturn (second) finger (8a).

The presence of a destiny line shows that, at least for the period the line is present, the

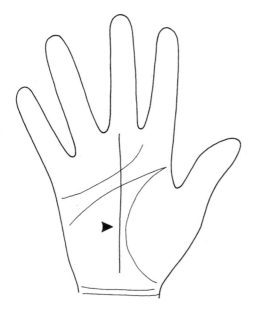

8a. Destiny line

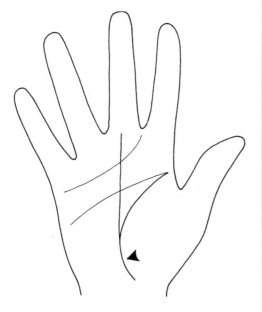

8b. Destiny line attached to life line

person will work to achieve a goal or dream. Consequently, it is usually necessary for any degree of success in life. It shows the person's direction in life, capacities, and attitudes toward success.

In the past, palmists believed that a long destiny line was an indication of great success. This is certainly not the case. Someone with a long destiny line but with no motivation is not going to get very far. Beggars in India often have long destiny lines, and it simply means that they have followed this particular career all of their lives.

The destiny line is also a sign of good fortune. People with it seem to be protected and are able to avoid some of the pitfalls that befall people without one. They usually manage to do the right thing, almost as if they are being guided to make the correct decision.

Absence of a Destiny Line

Someone without a destiny line may have a varied, interesting life but will certainly never be driven to succeed in any specific field. He or she will be like a ship without a rudder, buffeted first one way, then another. The absence of a destiny line is often found in the palms of misfits, criminals, and people who overindulge in alcohol or drugs.

Many years ago I read the palm of a wealthy self-made businessman and discovered he did not have a destiny line. It turned out that he had made his money by buying and selling anything he could buy cheaply and resell at a profit. One week he might be selling computers, the next week clothing, and so on. He was successful, but had become so by seizing every opportunity he found, rather than by following a specific career.

Starting Positions

If the destiny line starts attached to, or inside, the life line (8b) it denotes a strong family environment in the growing up years. We could say to this person:

"Your destiny line starts inside your life line. That makes for a major influence on you when you were very young, usually a family influence. Someone had an important affect on you, giving you a strong sense of right and wrong, and this influence remains with you always."

If the line starts away from the life line, nearer the center of the hand (8c), it denotes a more independent start in life. This could be an indication of a family that was not close. It may indicate your client went to a boarding school, or is perhaps an orphan. We might say:

"You have always liked to be a bit independent, right from the day you were born. You prefer to do things

8c. Independent start to destiny line

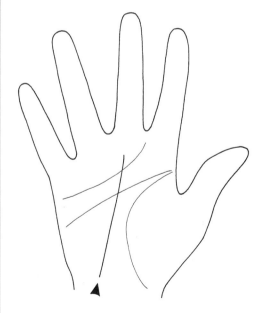

**8d. Destiny line starting
well across the palm**

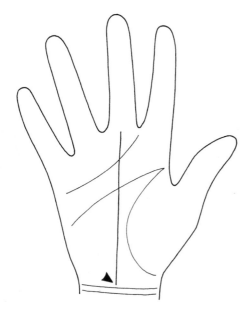

8e. Destiny line starting early in life

your way, and don't like being hemmed in or restricted."

If the destiny line starts well across the palm, further than halfway (8d), the independence is emphasized even more. Someone with their destiny line starting here is likely to enjoy a career dealing with the public in some sort of way.

If the destiny line starts virtually on the wrist (8e), the person decides what he or she wants to do and where he or she is going very early on in life. My doctor has this on his palms. He decided to study medicine as a very young child. When he left school, he went straight to university and then on to a career as a doctor. People like this are very fortunate. I have met plenty of retired people who never quite found out what they wanted to do with their lives!

Destiny Versus Fate Line

The destiny line is often called the fate line. I do not like this name as it seems to indicate that our entire lives are predetermined. I believe that we have the ability to change our lives, and hence our "fate," if we wish to. I have seen countless examples of this in my career. I also believe that some things cannot be changed as we all have limitations of different kinds and have to work within those limits. Some people are more intelligent than others, for instance. Many people are limited in what they can do by indifferent health. Geographical location can have a great bearing on what the person is able to do with his or her life.

The Bantus in Africa say that fate is "fan-shaped." A hunter miles from home has a choice of two paths to return to his village. If he takes one path he will be eaten by a lion, but if he takes the other path he will get home safely.

We all have decisions and choices in life, and just a few seconds can make an enormous difference. Years ago I lectured to a group of prison inmates and told them the Bantu belief that fate is fan-shaped. One of the inmates interjected and said that he believed it because if he had made a different decision he would not be in prison. As he said, "Thirty seconds changed my life."

Time on the Destiny Line

The destiny line shows time in an interesting way (8f). The first thirty-five years of the person's life are shown in the area between the wrist and the head line. Ages thirty-six to forty-nine are in the area between the head and heart lines, and the rest of the life is shown between the heart line and the fingers. Consequently, more than half of the entire length of the destiny line reveals the first thirty-five years of life, which may seem strange at first.

In palmistry, the first thirty-five years are the years in which people get their lives into order. It is amazing how many people finally work out what they want to do in life around the age of thirty-five, and this is shown by a change in the destiny line. The line may finish, and start again slightly separated from the original line. If there is an overlap, this indicates a time when the person was thinking about and planning for the change of direction.

Between the years of thirty-six and forty-nine the person is normally following a fairly set path. He or she is likely to be well settled in a particular career and be in a stable relationship. If this is not the case, it will be reflected in changes on the destiny line between the head and heart lines.

In palmistry, middle age starts around forty-nine, and many people's destiny lines stop at this point. This does not mean that they have no destiny after this age. It means that they become set in their ways. Someone with a des-

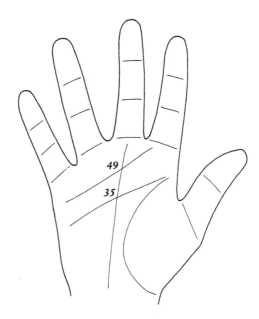

8f. Timing on the destiny line

tiny line continuing after the age of forty-nine will be experiencing new and different activities in his or her fifties, sixties, seventies—and maybe even beyond. This can often be an indication of longevity.

Many people have a destiny line that starts late. Rather than starting close to the wrist, it may start half way between the wrist and the head line. The point where it begins indicates the time when the person became motivated and started moving forward with purpose and direction.

Double Destiny Line

You will find some people with more than one destiny line (8g). This will be a fine line on the

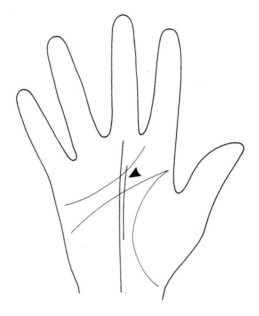

8g. Double destiny line

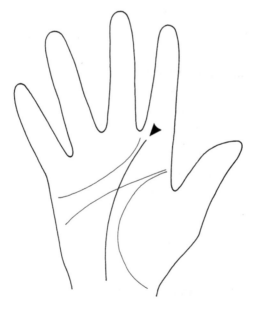

8h. Destiny line ending under first finger

thumb side of the destiny line, and indicates a time when the person was doing more than one important thing at a time. It may be an important career and an equally important hobby. It could be someone following up a career, but being just as involved with home and family. It could also indicate a "jack-of-all-trades"—someone who likes doing lots of different things at the same time.

Ending Positions

Where the destiny line ends is of great importance as well. If it curves slightly and ends directly under the first finger (8h) it gives an interest in politics, philosophy, and sometimes law. This is an unusual ending position.

The most common ending position is either under the second finger or between the second and third fingers (8i). This denotes someone who follows a fairly orthodox type of career. It could indicate someone in banking, teaching, a trade of some sort, a business person—any of the more usual type of occupations.

If it ends below the third finger (8j) it denotes a person involved in some form of creativity. It could indicate that the person is an artist, musician, interior decorator, or in any other creative career. I recently read the palm of a florist and she had a very well-defined destiny line that almost touched her third finger.

Occasionally, you will find a destiny line that comes right across the palm and ends under the little finger (8k). This person is a born communicator and could be involved in any career utilizing his or her skills in this area. He or she may, for instance, be an entertainer or sales person. Some years ago I read the palm of an auctioneer with this type of destiny line on his palm. Interestingly enough, he was a poor communicator in daily life, but in front of a crowd as an auctioneer, he could really perform and sell!

It is regarded as a fortunate sign if the destiny line ends in a trident formation (8l). These three small branches show that the person achieves great satisfaction out of life, and manages to successfully combine duty with pleasure.

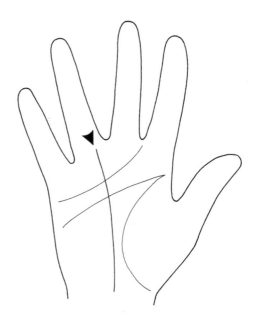

8j. Destiny line ending under third finger

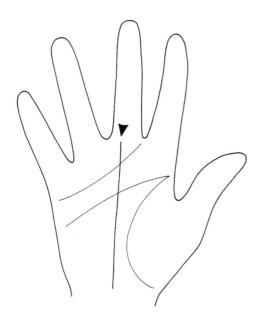

8i. Destiny line ending under second finger

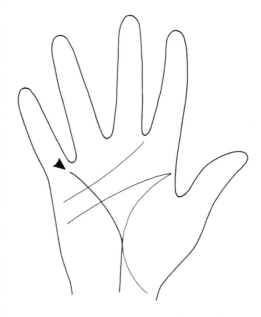

8k. Destiny line ending under fourth finger

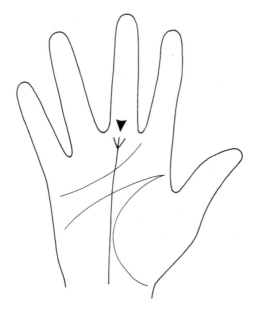

8l. Destiny line ending in trident

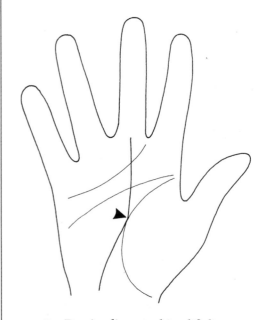

8n. Destiny line touching life line

Other Factors

Most destiny lines are not clear and well defined throughout their length. In some hands they almost fade away and then become strong again. In instances like this, where they fade for a time, it indicates that the person was not really sure where he or she was going at the time indicated.

You will often find destiny lines that have a break in them (8m). If the line stops and then starts again to one side of the original line, it is a sign of a change of career.

You will occasionally come across a destiny line that starts in the middle of the palm and then veers over and touches the life line before breaking free again (8n). This is a sign that

8m. Break in destiny line

family matters took precedence over the individual's own desires, and this person may have had to give up dreams of his own, such as going to college, because of the needs of someone close to him.

Squares on the destiny line (80) are always protective squares that shield the person from difficulties.

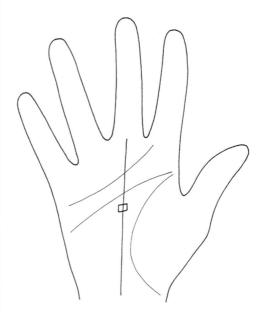

80. Protective square on destiny line

CHAPTER NINE

Minor Lines

As WELL AS the four major lines, there are a number of minor lines that need to be looked at. We do not read every line on the average hand, though, as many small lines are caused by nervous tension. Someone who is high-strung and nervous will have many more lines on his or her palm than someone who takes life as it comes. Consequently, when we see a hand that is completely covered with a multitude of fine lines, we know that the person uses up a great deal of nervous energy. You will also see hands

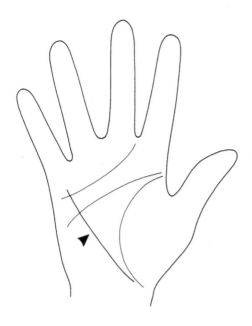

9a. Hepatica

with very few lines. These belong to people who do not worry unnecessarily and are basically easygoing.

Hepatica

The hepatica, or health line (9a), runs diagonally across the palm from inside the life line to near the start of the heart line. Oddly enough, it is an excellent sign not to have this line. People without the hepatica have abnormally good health, seldom even getting a cold in winter. The absence of this line indicates a good constitution and little stress.

If the line is present it should be as clear and well marked as possible. This is an indication that the owner pays attention to his own physical well-being and enjoys good health.

If the hepatica is clear and runs all the way from the life line to the mount of Mercury (the mound below the little finger) it is an indication of longevity. Someone with this line will pay attention to health matters when necessary, and will easily outlive most of his or her contemporaries.

A health line that varies in quality indicates periods of ill-health. This need not be a specific illness. The person may simply have periods of poor health.

If the health line has islands on it or is faint and indistinct, it is a sign of health problems. Usually, these can be timed by looking at the quality of the life line. Islands can be an indication of problems with the digestive system, and I have seen the quality of health lines improve enormously simply from a change of diet.

Breaks in the health line relate to periods of ill-health. A health line comprised of a series of tiny lines arranged in a step-like formation is an indication of lack of energy and stamina.

A star on the health line, particularly when sited close to the head line, is an indication of sterility, or of problems in childbirth.

A square on the health line is a protection for the period indicated. It is an extremely fortunate marking, indicating a complete recovery from the health problem.

The Sun Line

The sun line (9b) grants its possessors confidence, charm, and the potential for great success in the chosen career. Fame is a distinct possibility. This line is also known as the Apollo line. William Benham called it the "line of capability" as everyone with it is capable of great achievement. The presence of a sun line does not guarantee success in every sphere of life, however. It usually relates to career. Consequently, someone with this line would be likely to enjoy an extremely successful, rewarding career. At the same time, however, the person's home and family life may be a dismal failure.

The sun line runs parallel to the destiny line. Ideally, it should start close to the wrist and end beneath the third finger. This is very rare, however. Most sun lines are short and start near the head line and run toward the third finger. If the sun line starts near the wrist but is very short, it shows the person had a brilliant start in his or career, but was not able to maintain the momentum.

A strong sun line running clear and unmarked up the palm would indicate a life singularly free of problems and obstacles. Life is usually not like that, so people with a sun line almost always have defects on them.

An island on the sun line is an indication of scandal or loss of reputation. It is important to remember that a sun line offers the potential of great success, but it does not show the field of activity. A master criminal could have a sun line, indicating success in crime. Usually, though, people with a sun line are honest.

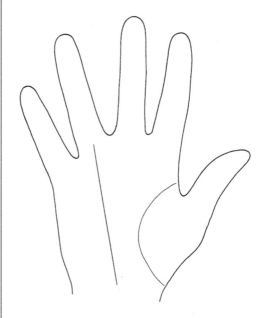

9b. Sun line

A cross on the sun line is an indication of financial loss or disappointment. If the sun line carries on beyond the cross it shows that the person recovers from the setback and carries on with a successful career.

A break in the sun line indicates a period where the person was not fully appreciated or recognized for his or her contributions.

Many breaks are an indication of great versatility, but the person is likely to spread his or her interests over too great an area. People with this are likely to lose interest in ventures just as they are about to succeed.

A square on the sun line is always a protection and helps the person preserve his or her good name. It protects the person from jealousy and malicious gossip.

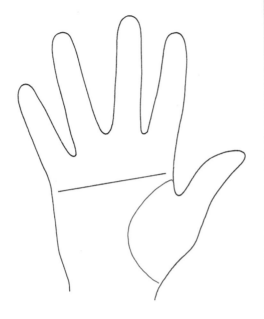

9c. Simian crease

The Simian Crease

The simian crease (9c) occurs when the head and heart lines combine to form one single line running across the palm. You will find it frequently on one hand, and very rarely on both.

People with this line can be extremely obstinate and have difficulties in relating with others. They are single-minded, highly tenacious, and have highly complex, intense emotions.

They are very reasonable when discussing an issue, but once their minds have been made up, they will refuse to discuss the matter further.

If this line is found on the minor hand, the person will have had a sheltered upbringing and will dislike responsibility. He or she will have one major interest in life and will pursue it with enormous intensity.

If found on the major hand, the person will be single-minded and have strong physical appetites. He or she will find it hard to relax and is likely to be a high achiever.

If the simian line is found on both hands the person will go his or her own way, requiring little input from others. He or she will be stubborn and unyielding. On a coarse hand, with no positive indications, the person could become involved in criminal activity. If there are positive indications on the palm, the person will harness his or her considerable energies into progressing in a career, or competing in sports or other physical activities.

A simian crease is common in those with Down's syndrome, though most people with it are perfectly normal and usually have a high intelligence.

Ring of Saturn

The ring of Saturn (9d) is a fine line which makes a semicircle below the second finger (the Saturn finger). It is usually a single line, but can be composed of two or three smaller lines that overlap each other. This line is rare, which is fortunate as it is a negative mark.

People with a ring of Saturn are plagued by self-doubt and negativity. They expect to fail and approach every activity with this in mind. In his book *Palmistry for All*, Cheiro described the ring of Saturn as "the most unfortunate mark ever to find." This is certainly an overstatement. This line can appear on some hands after a major tragedy, but will disappear once the person becomes more positive and starts looking ahead again. People with this line need to be treated gently and encouraged to set plans and goals for themselves, to help them move forward again.

Via Lasciva

The via lasciva (9e) is usually a straight line some three-quarters of the way down the palm from the fingers that heads across the palm towards the thumb. Occasionally, it can be slightly curved.

In the past this line had a bad name and was related to overindulgence in sex and drugs. Cheiro, in *Palmistry for All,* stated that it indicated "unbridled sensuality and passion."

Today it simply means that people with this line always need something exciting to look forward to. They need to be careful of alcohol and other drugs as they are influenced by these more than most people. This is no doubt how the name got its negative interpretation in the first place. Fortunately, most people with a via lasciva tend to dislike and avoid artificial stimulants.

The Teacher's Square

A small square directly under the first finger is known as the teacher's square (9f). It indicates that the person would be a natural teacher and has the ability to impart knowledge clearly to others. You will find this mark on the hands of

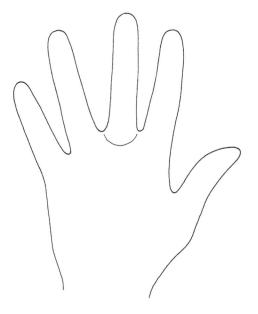

9d. Ring of Saturn

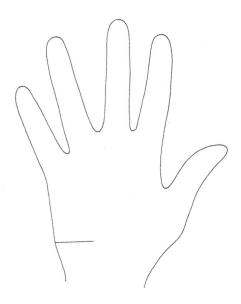

9e. Via lasciva

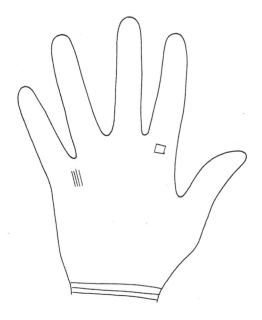

**9f., 9g., and 9h. The teacher's square,
rascettes, and medical stigmata**

all natural teachers. However, many people drift into teaching as a career and do not possess this square. You will find it on the hands of many people who would have made good teachers but chose another type of career instead. These people will still be making use of it whenever they have to explain something to someone else. Many people with a teacher's square become involved at some time in their life with private tuition, presenting seminars and workshops, or teaching a hobby or other interest.

The Rascettes

The rascettes (9g) are lines on the wrist at the very base of the palm. They are often called "bracelets." Traditionally, Gypsies regard each rascette as indicating twenty-five full years of life. Most people have three rascettes, so in the Gypsy interpretation almost everyone will live to the age of seventy-five!

The rascettes are ignored by most modern-day palmists, but there is one factor that has been known for thousands of years that has now been confirmed by scientists. If the top rascette arches upward into the palm it is an indication of gynecological problems and difficulties in childbirth. The ancient Greeks knew this. If the priests noticed a woman with the top rascette arching onto her palm, she became a vestal virgin at the temple and was not allowed to marry.

Medical Stigmata

The medical stigmata (9h) is a series of three or four tiny vertical lines below the little finger. Frequently, they are found slightly offset towards the ring finger. They are often called "Samaritan lines."

People with a medical stigmata have an empathy for all living things, and have a healing touch. They often gravitate toward one of the healing professions. Consequently, you will find this marking on the hands of good doctors, nurses, physiotherapists, naturopaths, veterinarians, and anyone else involved in the helping professions. Bear in mind that if someone has become attracted to one of these fields with the aim of making money rather than helping others, he or she will not have a medical stigmata.

The other minor lines—travel, intuition, relationships, children, money, the girdle of Venus, and the ring of Solomon—are dealt with in other chapters.

CHAPTER TEN

The Thumb

THE THUMB PLAYS an important role in palmistry. I have seen palmists in India doing most of their readings from an analysis of their clients thumbs, and there is good reason for this as the thumb can provide a great deal of useful information about the person's character. For instance, it can tell us how the person will make decisions and how he or she will carry them out.

Humanity is the only animal blessed with an opposing thumb. Chimpanzees come close, but their thumbs are very primitive compared to

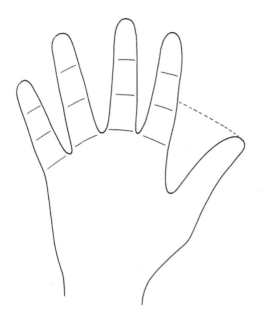

10a. Long thumb

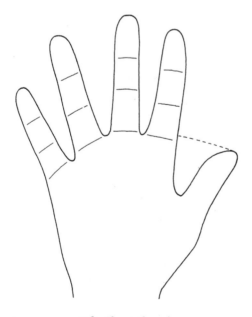

10b. Short thumb

ours. A unique feature of our thumbs is the radial nerve that is made of the same nerve fiber as the middle of our brains. This is the same nerve fiber that also runs through our spinal columns. This radial nerve is responsible for our superior reasoning capabilities that separate us from the rest of the animal kingdom.

Length of the Thumb

The larger the thumb, the greater the degree of success possible. Apparently Napoleon had an extremely large thumb, which is not surprising. It is an interesting exercise to watch people's hands on television, and often you will find actors playing roles that they could never have achieved in real life. An example of this would be someone with a small thumb playing the part of a successful business tycoon. In India, it is believed that the size of the thumb has a direct relationship with the degree of success the person will have in life. I find this interpretation a bit too fatalistic, but there is no doubt that people with large thumbs usually reach the top positions. This is because they are more motivated, ambitious, and persistent than people with small thumbs. Charlotte Wolff did a survey of the thumbs of successful individuals and found that most had thumbs of normal length. Certainly, people with long thumbs will try much harder to get what they want than people with short thumbs.

If you ever find someone with an extremely long thumb (10a), you will have found someone capable of a leadership role in any situation. This person will be intelligent, decisive, and have a strong will.

People with short thumbs (10b) are lacking in will. They can be stubborn, though often for no apparent reason.

People with medium length thumbs (reaching to at least halfway up the lowest phalange of the first finger) (10c) are fair and can stand up for themselves. They show common sense and possess reasonable willpower.

If the thumb is broad (10d), looking at it from the nail side, the person will be prepared to do whatever is necessary to get what he or she wants.

Someone with a thick-looking thumb (10e) will be extremely blunt and forthright. This person will be stubborn and want his or her own way at any cost.

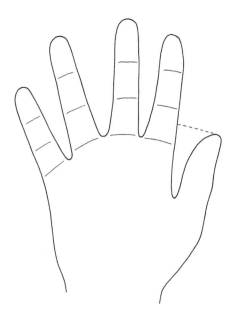

10c. Average thumb

Sections of the Thumb

The fingers and thumb are all divided into three sections, known as phalanges (10f). The joints divide the fingers into three parts, whilst the thumb appears to have just two sections. The mount of Venus, which is the fleshy mound at the base of the thumb surrounded by the life line, is called the third phalange.

Ideally, the first and second phalanges of the thumb should be equal in length (10g). The first phalange, containing the thumbnail, represents will, and the second phalange represents logic. Someone with first and second

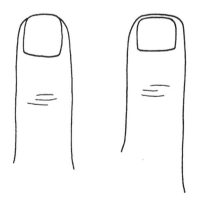

10d. Broad thumb and 10e. Stubborn thumb

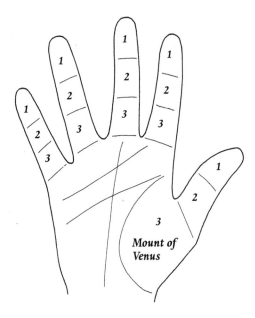

10f. Finger and thumb phalanges

Mount of Venus

phalanges of the same length will possess an equal amount of logic and willpower. He or she will be able to come up with a good idea and then have the necessary drive and energy to carry it out.

If the first phalange is longer than the second (10h), the individual will have more willpower than logic. This person will make plenty of mistakes, but will regroup each time and carry on until he or she reaches his goal. This combination gives great determination. He or she will be prepared to work hard and long, but can also be domineering.

Most people have the second phalange longer than the first (10i). This means there is more logic than willpower present. Someone

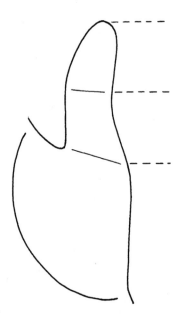

10g. First and second phalanges equal in length

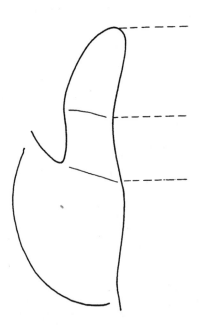

10h. More will power than logic

with this combination will have lots of ideas, but somehow never quite gets around to doing them. They will think, and think, and then think some more. Everything is present except the motivation to act. That, of course, is why so many of us achieve only a minute fraction of what we are capable of doing. Too much logic, too little will.

Angle of the Thumb

The average thumb is held at an angle of about forty-five degrees to the hand (10j). This is an indication of reasonable open-mindedness and the ability to conform to society's standards. Speaking generally, the wider the angle of the thumb, the more generous the person will be. Consequently, this angle is known as the "angle of generosity" (10k).

If the thumb forms a narrower angle (10l) it makes the person more selfish. He or she is likely to be small-minded and mean. This person's outlook on the world will be very limited.

If the angle is wider than average it indicates someone who is outgoing, energetic, and has the potential to influence and sway others. He or she will be adventurous and willing to try new and different things.

If the thumb is habitually held out from the hand it is a sign of a relaxed, outgoing, carefree person.

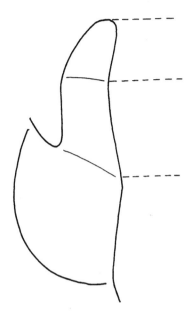

10i. More logic than willpower

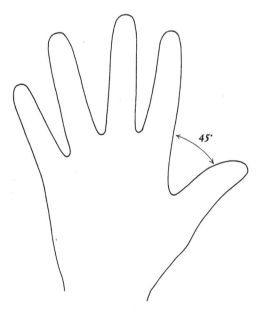

10j. Average angle of the thumb

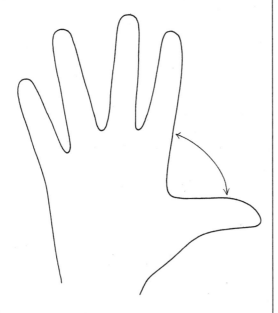

10k. Wide angle of the thumb

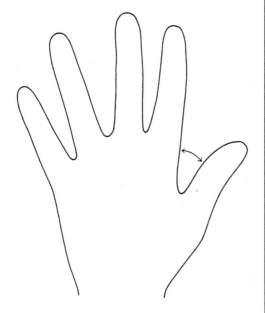

10l. Narrow angle of the thumb

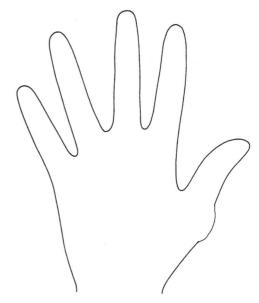

10m. Angle of practicality

Angle of Practicality

The angle of practicality is an angle formed on the outside of the thumb where it joins the palm (10m). You will find many people have virtually no angle at this point at all, but other people have large bulges at this spot. The larger the "bump" at this point, the more practical the person will be. People with this have manual dexterity and enjoy working with their hands.

This angle is sometimes known as the "angle of time" as it gives the person a special sense of time. This can create someone who is always punctual, and in a comedian, for instance, it would give him or her a good sense of timing.

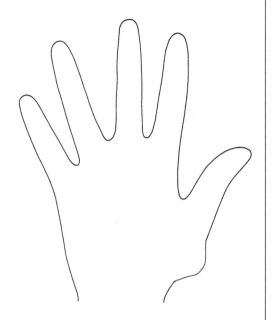

10n. Angle of pitch

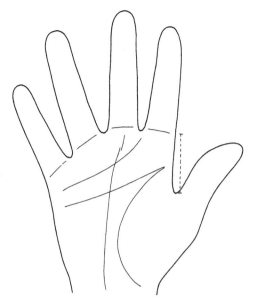

10o. High-set thumb

Angle of Pitch

The angle of pitch is found at the very base of the palm below the thumb where it joins the wrist (10n). It gives the person a good ear for music and a sense of rhythm.

Good musicians, dancers, and singers will all have good angles of practicality and pitch. The angle of practicality gives them good timing, while the angle of pitch gives them a good ear for music and a sense of rhythm. You will notice these in photographs of all kinds of musicians ranging from the classics to pop. Next time you see a photograph of Elvis Presley take a close look at his hands. You will see that both of these angles were prominent in his hands.

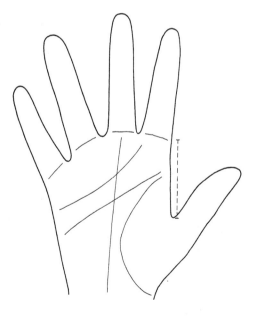

10p. Low-set thumb

10q. Square tip

10r. Spatulate tip

Setting of the Thumb

Thumbs can be set in different places, and are thus regarded as being "high-set" or "low-set."

A high-set thumb (10o) is one that starts well up the hand from the wrist. People with this setting have originality and are outward-looking. People with low-set thumbs (10p) are more cautious and restrained.

Most people have thumbs set somewhere between these two extremes.

Tips of the Thumb

Few palmists nowadays use D'Artepigny's classification system for the hand, but the terms he devised are still used in examining the tips of the thumb and fingers.

If the tip of the thumb is square (10q) in appearance the individual will be practical, down-to-earth, and have a sense of fair play.

If the tip is spatulate (10r) the person will be busy and active.

If the tip is conic (10s) the person will be refined and sensitive. Often the conic tip is connected to a second phalange that appears "waisted" and curves inward on both sides (10t). This means that the person is diplomatic and tactful. When he or she says, "No," it will be done in a very pleasant way, so as not to hurt the other person's feelings.

If the tip is tapered (10u) the individual is a subtle thinker who will be able to tell you bad news in an extremely gentle way.

10s. Conic tip

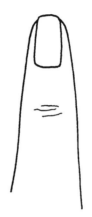

10u. Tapered thumb

10t. Waisted thumb

10v. Broad-tipped thumb

10w. "Murderer's thumb"

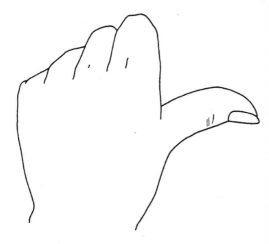

10x. Flexible thumb

If the tip is broad and flat (10v) in appearance the individual will be careful and firm. If the tip section is flattened as well, appearing almost as a knob on top of the second phalange, you will be looking at what is known as the "murderer's thumb" (10w). As this trait often runs through families, it is usually inherited. People with this type of thumb can be patient for a long while, but then something trivial will make them react violently. Doubtless, this is how the "murderer's thumb" got its name.

Flexibility

Thumbs are either firm or flexible. If it bends backward from the joint it is regarded as being flexible (10x). Someone with this characteristic will be easy-going, positive, and flexible. He or she will also give in under pressure, rather than create a scene.

If the thumb is stiff and does not bend back at the joint it is classified as being firm. Someone with this type of thumb will be determined, reliable, and stubborn. He or she will be unyielding and not give in under pressure.

At one time in my life I worked as a salesman and this knowledge was very useful to me. If I was dealing with a customer with a flexible thumb I could push to make the sale. When dealing with someone with a firm thumb I would not push, but would gently retreat and try again later. If I had tried to push the firm-thumbed clients into a sale I would not have succeeded, and would have created obstacles to later success.

CHAPTER ELEVEN

Indian Thumb Reading

I HAVE BEEN fascinated with thumb reading ever since I had my thumb read in Bombay more than thirty years ago. I was making my living as a palmist at the time, and was amazed at how this palm reader totally ignored the rest of my hand and gave me a reading based solely on my thumb. I have had my thumbs read on several occasions since, and have always been amazed at the accuracy and detail that the thumbs can provide. Unfortunately, the only books that taught the art of thumb reading were in Pali, Sanskrit, and Tamil. At times, people

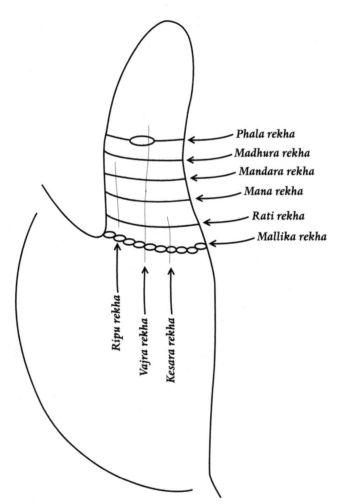

11a. Indian thumb reading

offered to teach me the art, but I never learned enough to be able to make practical use of it.

A few years ago, I was able to spend a few days with my good friend Sameer Upadhyay in New Delhi. One of the many things we talked about was the basic principles of thumb reading. It is thanks to Sameer that I have been able to add the extra insights gained from thumb reading to my palmistry, and I am grateful to him for his kindness and generosity.

Type of Thumb

The palmist feels and examines the thumb to determine its type. This follows the same principles we use in the West. If the thumb is stiff and rigid, the person is stubborn and unyielding. If the thumb bends back easily, he or she is flexible and gives in under pressure.

The tips of the thumb are classified using D'Arpentigny's system. Again, this is the same method that we use in the West. D'Arpentigny's classification system for hands is still commonly used in India. Nowadays, in the West we use it mainly for determining thumb types.

Dermatoglyphics

The skin ridge patterns at the tip of the thumb are examined.

Lines of the Thumb

There are nine lines (or *rekha*) that can appear on the thumb. It is unusual to find someone with all nine, but everyone has at least two. These are the lines that divide the phalanges. There is one between the willpower and logic phalanges, and another between the logic phalange and the mount of Venus.

Horizontal Lines

The horizontal lines begin on the Jupiter finger side of the thumb, and ideally stretch all the way across the thumb. We want all of these lines to be as smooth as possible.

Phala Rekha (Wheat Line)

The *phala rekha* is commonly referred to as the wheat line. Occasionally, it is called the rice line. The word *phala* means "a fruit," or "the result of an outcome." This can be related to karma. In fact, *karma-phala* means "result of an action." Consequently, a good deed creates a positive outcome. Likewise, an evil deed ultimately reaps a negative outcome. This line is also sometimes referred to as the *pushpa* (flower) *rekha*, as it looks like a flower.

The phala rekha is the line that divides the willpower and logic phalanges of the thumb. It is rare to find it absent on the thumb. Its presence indicates that the person will always have enough to eat. If it appears to contain a grain of wheat or rice, it indicates that the person will lead a happy and fulfilled life.

Usually, the wheat line is made up of two interconnected lines, representing the man and the woman. This line usually starts as a single line, but is quickly joined by another line, which represents his or her partner in life. Consequently, the time when the two people became involved can be determined by studying this line. Disturbances in this line usually relate to problems inside relationships.

If the wheat line is wavy, or uneven, at the start, it indicates that the person had a difficult childhood. If it is wavy in the middle, it indicates problems in middle life. Naturally, wavy lines at the end indicate a difficult old age.

Mallika Rekha

Mallika is a small white flower, similar in appearance to jasmine. Traditionally, it is offered to Lord Siva. The *mallika rekha* divides the phalange of logic and the mount of Venus. It should be clear and well marked. This indicates a happy and contented home and family life. This line often appears as a continual chain. This gives the person courage and strength of character.

Black dots on this line indicate financial problems between family members. If the line is noticeably thicker than the wheat line, it is a sign that the person will have problems in finding the right relationship, and in sustaining it, once found. If this line has gaps in it, it is a sign that the person will experience considerable ups and downs in life.

The other four horizontal lines are all found inside the logic phalange. If all four are present, they effectively divide this phalange into fifths.

The first three (madhura, mandara, and mana) are seen only occasionally. The final line inside the logic phalange (*rati rekha*) is found frequently.

Madhura Rekha

Madhura means "having sweetness." *The madhura rekha* is the one closest to the wheat line. This line should be fine, yet easy to see. This indicates that the bearer will be compassionate and easy to get along with.

Mandara Rekha

Mandara is the name of a mythological mountain. It is also a synonym for heaven and mirror. The *mandara rekha* line reveals an interest in travel. It gives the person an inbuilt restlessness that virtually ensures that he or she will travel at some stage.

Mana Rekha

Mana is an abstract term describing the place where our thoughts, feelings, emotions, and desires reside. The *mana rekha* is not a positive line. It shows that the person is likely to have affairs outside of his or her marriage.

Rati Rekha

Rati was the wife of Kamadev, the Hindu god of love. The word *rati* describes the act of making love. The rati rekha needs to be read in conjunction with the lines of romantic attachment on the side of the palm below the Mercury finger. The rati rekha shows the degree of satisfaction and happiness the person derives from his relationship.

Ideally, this line should be clear, well marked, and unbroken. An island on this line shows that the person's partner will suffer ill-health at the time indicated. If the line is cut in half, the person will experience happiness until middle age, and then problems will develop. These difficulties usually relate to the health of the partner. If the line carries on after the split, it means that the problems have been overcome.

If the rati rekha consists of a series of broken lines, it is a sign that the person will lead a celibate life.

Vertical Lines

There are three vertical lines that run lengthwise up the thumb. The *vajra rekha,* which divides the thumb in half, is always the longest of these.

Vajra Rekha

The *vajra* is an ancient weapon that looks like the metallic part of a spear. It was the primary weapon used by Lord Indra, the god of rains and lightning. Lightning is said to be the flash of Indra's vajra. The vajra rekha is a fine line that is found on the Jupiter finger side of the thumb, heading upward from the malika rekha. Occasionally, it starts inside the mount of Venus. This line is commonly known as the diamond line, as people with it have the potential to become extremely wealthy. In fact, vajra is a synonym for diamond and steel. However, for this to occur, the line needs to be clear and prominent in the hand. If the kesara rekha is also strong, the person will make money without much effort. If the vajra rekha is wavy in formation, the person will make his or her fortune in speculative ways.

Kesara Rekha

The word *kesara* has several meanings. It is the name for saffron, which is used for flavoring foods. The gynoecium part (pistil) of a flower is called kesara. The mane of an Indian lion is also known as kesara.

The *kesara rekha* parallels the vajra rekha on the opposite side of the thumb. It is usually a short line that starts on the mount of Venus and finishes on the mallika rekha.

The presence of this line indicates the gradual growth of the family's fortune. When it is fine and hard to see, it shows that the person will do well financially over a long period of time. When it is thick and easy to see, the person will make his or her fortune more quickly. If this line is clear and well marked, and extends up the thumb to the wheat line, it is a sign that the person comes from a wealthy family. He or she will usually be interested in the arts. People without this line find it hard to progress financially.

Ripu Rekha

The *ripu rekha* starts on the mount of Venus and runs up the middle of the thumb to the wheat line. Occasionally, it goes beyond this into the phalange of willpower.

The word *ripu* means "enemy." Consequently, this line is often known as the enmity line, and has a negative effect on any of the lines it crosses.

As well as determining the type of thumb, the dermatoglyphics and the lines, Indian palmists also look for different symbols and shapes formed by the lines and skin ridge patterns. A fish, for example, shows that the person will do well in life. A crab, or scorpion, shows that the person will remain a servant. The number of possibilities is unlimited, and you need a good imagination, not to mention good eyesight, to find them. However, this takes us away from serious palmistry, which is why I am not including them here.

I have found knowledge of the nine lines in the thumb a useful adjunct in my practice. They provide insights that cannot be found in any other way. Do not concern yourself with them until you feel confident in reading the main lines of the hand. Take notes and ask questions when using these lines. This is one area of palmistry that is totally new in the West and you may well be able to make valuable and original contributions by careful observation.

CHAPTER TWELVE

The Fingers

WE HAVE ALREADY briefly discussed finger lengths in our initial classification of the hand. Before going on to describe each finger individually, here are a few things to look for on all of the fingers.

First, look to see how the fingers are held when the hands are shown to you. If the fingers are all close together (3a) it is an indication of caution and timidity. If the fingers are held apart from each other (12a) it is a sign of openness and confidence.

On the base phalange, which is the section nearest the palm, you may notice some fine

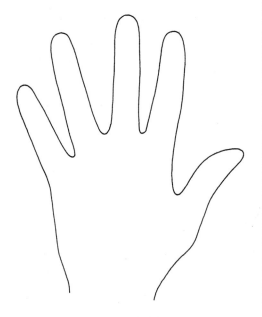

12a. Fingers held apart

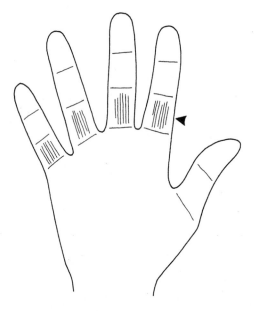

12b. Strain lines

vertical lines (12b). These are known as strain lines. They appear when the person is in need of a few days rest. Incidentally, even a good night's sleep can affect these lines. They are caused by a number of factors. Stress, going too long without a vacation, overtiredness, and generally overdoing things all contribute to creating these lines. When I see them I always advise the person to have a short break, and to make sure that it is a restful holiday, as some people seem to work even harder on vacation than they do normally!

Horizontal lines on the first, or nail, phalange are called stress lines (12c). Strain lines can come and go very quickly, but stress lines take a long time to appear and just as long to go away again. They are caused by continued stress over a long period. When they are present, it is time for the person to get out of the stressful situation, have a vacation, and reevaluate his or her life. These lines can indicate the possibility of future health problems caused by stress. When you see very faint stress lines on a hand, it is an indication of the lines gradually appearing or disappearing. When you see this you will know that the person has either been under a great deal of stress in the recent past or is currently experiencing it.

The fingers should be straight. If they curve one way or another they are gaining support from other fingers, and this means the person is underrating himself or herself in whatever area is indicated.

The Phalanges

The fingers are divided into three sections, known as phalanges. Ideally, each phalange should be similar in length to the other phalanges on the same finger. If one phalange is longer than the other two, the person will be using the energies of that phalange at the expense of the others. If a phalange is very short, the energy is dormant and not being utilized. As in everything else in palmistry, we aim for balance.

The tip phalange relates to intuition and spirituality (12d). If all the tip phalanges are long it shows that the person will be thoughtful and interested in the meaning of life.

The middle phalange relates to the intellect (12d). If these phalanges are all long the person will be good at business matters.

The base phalange relates to the material aspects of life (12d). If this phalange is long, thick, and puffy in appearance, the person will be self-indulgent and greedy. Make sure that you do not mistake this for padded base phalanges that are slightly spongy to the touch. This is an indication that the person likes good food, and is usually an excellent cook. Even if this person does not like cooking, he or she will be better than average at it, and will always appreciate well-prepared, tasty meals.

Finger Joints

Fingers have either smooth joints or knotty ones. Someone with knotty joints (fingers where the

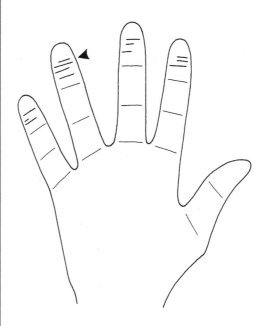

12c. Stress lines

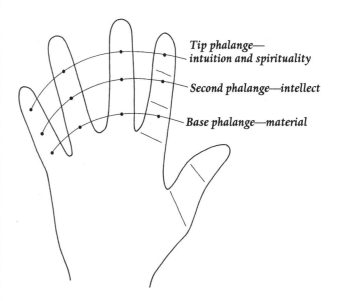

Tip phalange—intuition and spirituality

Second phalange—intellect

Base phalange—material

12d. Finger phalanges

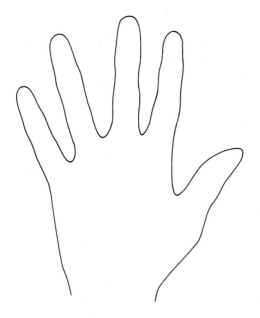

12e. Knotty joints

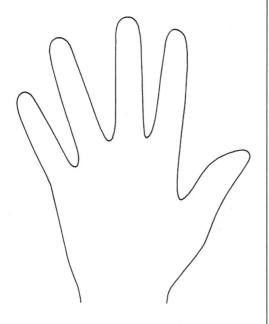

12f. Smooth joints

joints are very visible) (12e) will like to analyze things and work them out thoroughly before acting. Some authorities relate knotty joints to concentric circles. The thought enters at the tip of the finger, comes down and when it finds a knotty joint goes around and around several times before proceeding. If you know someone who likes to argue and discuss everything to the nth degree, you can be sure that person has knotty joints.

Smooth joints are virtually invisible (12f). Someone with smooth joints will not analyze things the way his or her knotty-jointed friend does. He or she will rely more on intuition and inspiration. There are many more smooth-jointed people in the world than knotty-jointed ones. It relates very much to the way the person uses his or her brain.

The knot between the tip and second phalange is known as the "knot of philosophy." Someone with this particular knot on each finger will not accept anything without a great deal of prior thought.

The knot between the second and base phalange is called the "knot of order." Someone with this knot will be systematic and orderly and have a place for everything. This can sometimes seem contradictory, as the person may be basically untidy yet insist that papers be correctly filed.

Setting of the Fingers

The fingers can be mounted on the hand in four main ways.

If the setting of the fingers creates a gentle curved arch (12g) it shows someone who is well balanced and sees him or herself as an individual in the world. This person does not consider him or herself to be better or worse than anyone else.

An arch that is tent-shaped (12h), with both the Mercury (little) and Jupiter (first) fingers lower than the others, reveals someone who is unsure of him or herself and uncertain of his or her abilities.

If the fingers are set in a straight line the person will have plenty of confidence and be very proud of his or her abilities. If the first and second fingers are also the same length he or she will be vain, arrogant, and ruthlessly ambitious.

If all the fingers are set in a slight curve, but with the little finger set noticeably lower (12i) we have a formation that is very common today. It is known as the "dropped" little finger. This is a sign that the person will experience a number of setbacks along the path through life, and will have to try and extricate him or herself each time. Things will go well for a long while but then the person will suddenly be dropped into something that would have been difficult to foresee. It is a sign of learning the hard way.

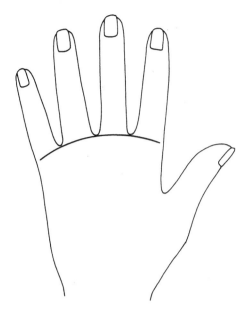

12g. Curved arch

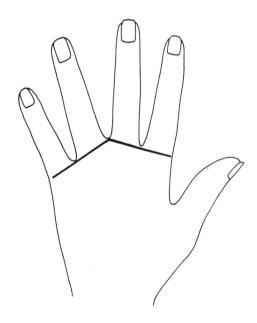

12h. Tented arch

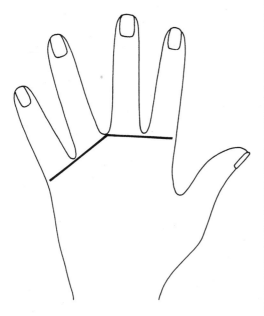

12i. "Dropped" little finger

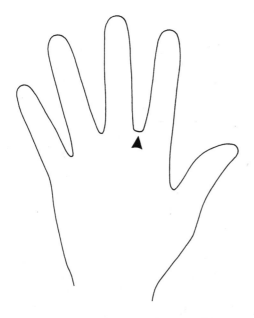

12j. Space between first and second fingers

Spacing of the Fingers

When you ask someone to show you their palms they will usually display them with the fingers held slightly apart. This shows that they are reasonably independent thinkers.

If the fingers are held tightly together you have someone who will conform in every possible way. This person will come up with very few independent ideas.

Someone with very wide gaps between the fingers will be a nonconformist who enjoys shocking and surprising others.

When there is a gap between the first and second fingers (12j) the person will be an independent thinker who is able to make decisions. It is a good combination for a manager or supervisor to have.

It is rare to find a gap between the second and third fingers (12k). This is a sign of someone who values freedom and is hard to tie down.

A gap between the last two fingers (third and fourth) (12l) is a sign of someone who likes to make up his or her own mind. This individual can be rather unconventional in his or her thinking and this can lead to difficulties in close relationships.

Tip Shapes

The shape of the fingertips conforms very much to D'Artepigny's system of classification of the entire hand. There are three main types: square, spatulate, and conic (12m, 12n, and 12o.). These are often found in hands of the same type. For instance, conic-shaped fingers are most often found on conic shaped hands. However, you are more likely to find hands which contain a mixture of tips. The forefinger may be square, the second finger conic, and the third finger spatulate.

If the tips are conic, the person will think in a practical, yet idealistic way. The person will be easy-going, quick-thinking, and sensitive.

Pointed tips are an extreme form of the conic. Someone with these tips will be highly impressionable and intuitive. He or she will be inspirational, temperamental, and have a nervous disposition.

Someone with square tips will be practical and enjoy working to a set routine. This person will like order and be a slow, careful, methodical thinker. He or she is likely to prefer the tried and true over something new and different.

Spatulate tips, which flare at the ends, are a sign of someone who is practical and inventive. He or she will be restless and enjoy change and wide open spaces. This person will be intelligent, unconventional, and enjoy discussing new ideas.

Someone with mixed finger tips (a range of different types all on the one hand) will be versatile and interested in a wide range of different subjects. He or she will also be adaptable and able to fit in to any situation. You will usually find that even in mixed hands one type will predominate and the person will have more of the qualities of that type than the others. It is common for people with mixed hands to follow an orthodox career using the predominant type of tip, but utilize the other tips in hobbies and interests.

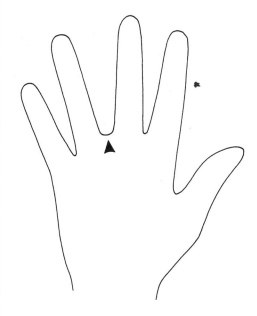

12k. Space between second and third fingers

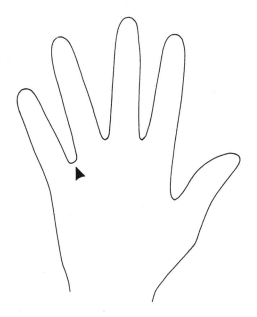

12l. Space between third and fourth fingers

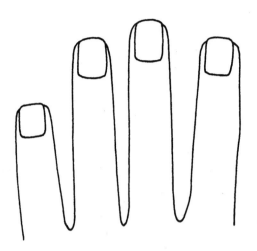

12m. Square tips

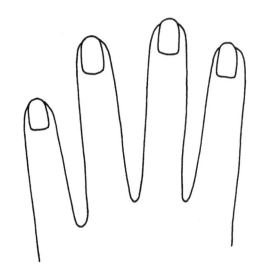

12o. Conic tips

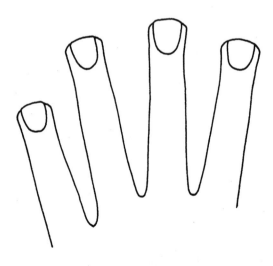

12n. Spatulate tips

Flexibility of the Fingers

Whilst looking at the hand push gently on the tips and see if the fingers are tense or flexible. As always, we are looking for balance, and are ideally wanting fingers that are supple, but not overly flexible.

If the fingers are tense the person is blocking energy and repressing himself or herself. If the fingers are overly flexible the person will give in far too easily. Rigid fingers belong to someone who is firm and fixed in outlook. Supple fingers provide a balance. The person will give in small ways, but will still be able to stand up for him or herself when necessary.

Check each finger, as often you will find some fingers are tense whilst others on the same palm are supple. This is a sign that the person is deliberately blocking the talents and attributes of the fingers that are tensed.

between the first and third fingers. It is often easier to gauge the respective lengths of each finger from the back, rather than from the palm side.

Length of the Fingers

It is necessary at times to check the length of one finger as compared to another. This is usually done

CHAPTER THIRTEEN

The Mercury Finger

You HAVE NO DOUBT already noticed that a number of parts of the hand are named after different planets. The little finger is named after the planet Mercury. Mercury was the winged messenger, and the little finger is the finger of communication. It also relates to activity and sex.

This finger should reach up to about the first joint of the third finger (13a). If longer than this, the communication skills are enhanced, but if shorter, the person will have difficulty in expressing his or her thoughts. If it is very short (13b) the person will be emotionally immature,

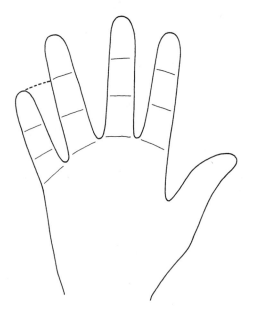

13a. Average-length Mercury finger

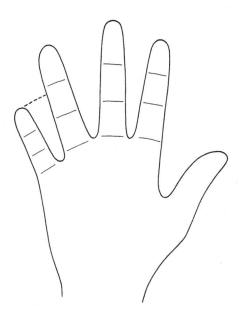

13b. Short Mercury finger

which is certain to create sexual problems. The length of this finger is complicated in that in many people it is set low on the palm. The other three fingers may all be set in a reasonably straight line on the edge of the palm, whilst the little finger is set down a step. The bigger the step, the greater the ups and downs the person will experience. This setting of the little finger is known as a "dropped" little finger (12i). When it is present you can say:

> "You have what is known as a dropped little finger, as it is set so much lower than the others. This means that everything will go beautifully for you for a long time, and then, all of a sudden, you will be dropped into a situation and have to climb out again. It means learning the hard way, learning through experience."

Like all the other fingers, the Mercury finger should be straight. This shows that the person is basically honest. If it is bent, or even slightly twisted in appearance, it is an indication of potential dishonesty. I have noticed this formation on the hands of a number of money changers in India! When I see it on a hand, I always advise the person to be very careful and honest in all financial dealings.

The Phalanges

Now we look at the relative lengths of the three phalanges. The tip phalange governs all verbal communication and is by far the longest on most people's hands (13c). People with long tip phalanges on this finger express themselves best by talking, and it is a very desirable quality for anyone who makes their living with this form of communication. Sales people, radio and television announcers, teachers, and anyone else who makes a career out of talking will have a large first phalange.

If the tip phalange is short (13d) the person will find it hard to learn and will have major problems in expressing him or herself.

Frequently, the second phalange is very small (13e). This phalange governs written communication. People with very small second phalanges will do anything to avoid putting their thoughts

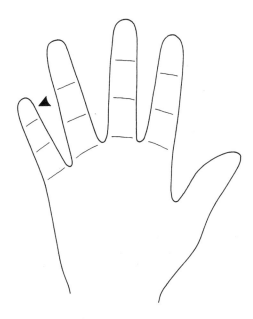

13d. Short tip on Mercury finger

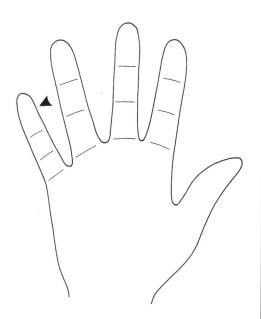

13c. Long tip on Mercury finger

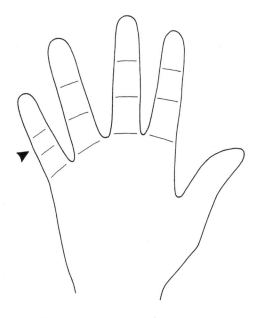

13e. Short second phalange on Mercury finger

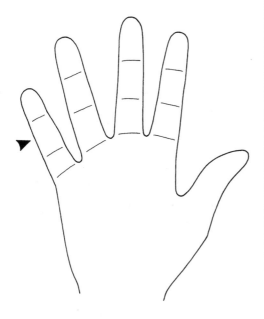

13f. Long second phalange on Mercury finger

on paper. People with large second phalanges (13f) usually enjoy expressing themselves in this way. You will find a good second phalange on writers, of course, but you will also find it on people who write good letters, or who can explain something more easily by writing it down rather than verbally describing it. Often these people are aware that they have ability in this area, but do nothing to develop it.

A good-sized second phalange also shows that the person can start something and then carry it through to fruition without losing interest halfway through. Conversely, if this section is very small the person will have a lack of organizational skills.

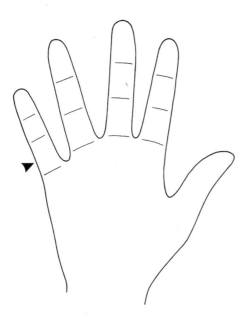

13g. Long base phalange on Mercury finger

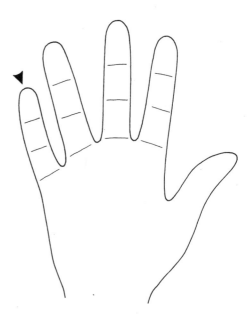

**13h. Curving Mercury finger—
"finger of sacrifice"**

The third, or base, phalange relates to the material world—specifically money. If this phalange is the largest (13g) the person will love money for its own sake. This individual will be highly persuasive and also be prepared to bend the truth when it suits his or her needs.

known as the "finger of sacrifice" and is an indication that the person will sublimate his or her own ambitions to help others. This formation is often found on the hands of nurses and caregivers of all sorts. If I needed someone to look after me, I would try and find someone with a "finger of sacrifice!"

Curving Finger

Every now and again you find a little finger that curves towards the Apollo finger (13h). This is

CHAPTER FOURTEEN

The Apollo Finger

THE THIRD FINGER is called the Apollo or sun finger. It represents beauty and creativity. This finger should reach halfway up the fingernail of the Saturn (second) finger and be about the same length as the Jupiter (first) finger (14a). If it is longer than this (14b) the person will have a highly creative nature. A long Apollo finger is also often related to gambling. This can be expressed by taking chances, rather than actual gambling at cards or horses.

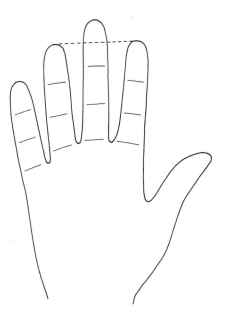

14a. Ideal length Apollo finger

A Curving Apollo Finger

The Apollo finger should be straight. If it curves towards the Mercury finger (14c) it is an indication that the person underrates his or her creative ability. If someone with this formation did something creative it would be of a higher standard than he or she would think.

If the Apollo finger curves the other way, towards the Saturn finger (14d), it is an indication that the person has given up his or her creativity for something much more mundane. You would find this on the hands of a talented artist who found it hard to make a living out of art, and gave it up to work as a clerk.

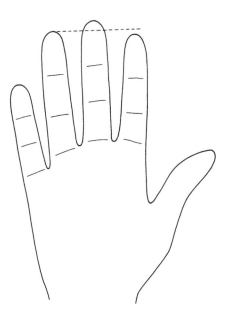

14b. Long Apollo finger

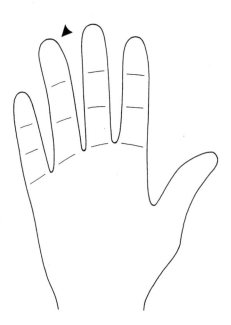

14c. Apollo finger curving toward Mercury finger

The Phalanges

Most people have phalanges of about equal length on the Apollo finger. They appreciate nice things and comfortable, pleasant surroundings.

If the tip phalange is longer than the others (14e) it denotes someone with high ideals and beautiful thoughts. It can sometimes indicate creative ability. You will have to look at other factors to confirm this, and we will cover these later on. However, as you already know about creative, imaginative head lines, it would pay to have another look at the head line to confirm this creativity. As often as possible, find points of agreement on the palm before making bald pronouncements. People are highly complex, and something may be indicated on one part of the hand but have its direct opposite shown somewhere else. If we are aware of this contradiction before we speak, we can modify it. "At times you are . . . , but at other times . . . ."

Frank Lloyd Wright, the famous architect, is a good example of someone with a long tip phalange on this finger who made brilliant use of this potential by creating a whole new style of architecture.

The second phalange is frequently longer than the first (14f). This denotes that the person has extremely good taste, and would do well in a field where this could be used. An interior decorator would be a good example of this. (In contrast, an interior designer would likely have a long tip phalange.) Someone with a long second phalange will possess originality

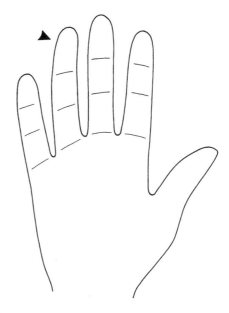

14d. Apollo finger curving toward Saturn finger

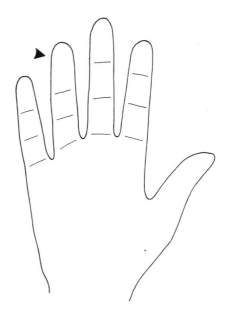

14e. Long first phalange on Apollo finger

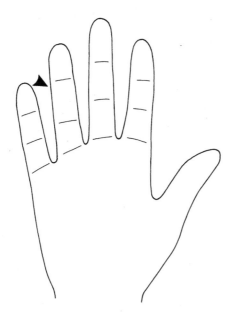

**14f. Long second phalange on Apollo finger
toward Saturn finger**

and will apply it with good common sense. Someone with a good tip on the Mercury finger, denoting verbal skills, plus a good second phalange on the Apollo finger (good taste) would be extremely good at selling things they personally found attractive. I have seen this combination on the hands of a number of antique dealers. They like antiques and are good at selling them.

The base phalange is least likely to be the longest. If it is, it shows that the person has a materialistic approach to life with little feeling for beauty and aesthetic values. These people will want to achieve success in the material world and then surround themselves with extravagant clothes and possessions to make a good show. The emphasis is on comfort and pleasure.

CHAPTER FIFTEEN

The Saturn Finger

THE SECOND FINGER is known as the Saturn finger. It governs common sense, restrictions, and restraint. It also relates to duty and service. This finger is named after Saturn, a rather aloof and gloomy god who gave his name to "saturnine." If this finger is the strongest finger on the hand the person will be extremely saturnine and his or her intellect would always rule over emotion.

This should be the longest finger on the hand. If it is too long in relation to the other fingers the person will find it hard to fit in with others and

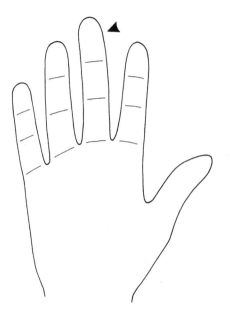

15a. Saturn finger curving toward Apollo finger

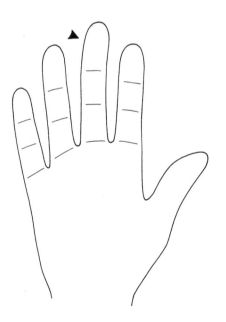

15b. Saturn finger curving toward Jupiter finger

will prefer being on his or her own. He or she will be aloof and unsociable. If this finger is short the person will be careless and lack a sense of responsibility. Most people have Saturn fingers that are neither long nor short.

Curving Saturn Finger

The Saturn finger is the finger most likely to be curved. If it curves over the Apollo finger (15a), the person holds back creatively, underrating his or her capabilities. He or she will need plenty of encouragement from family and friends. Along with this, he or she will be frequently tempted to play rather than "dig in" and work.

It is more serious if it curves the other way, over the first finger (15b). This finger governs the person's ego, and a curving Saturn finger is an indication that the person underrates his or her entire being. This can lead to an inferiority complex.

Finger Cling

When the Saturn finger is straight, but is held almost touching an adjacent finger when the hand is held open, we have what is termed a "finger cling."

If the Saturn finger clings to the Apollo finger the person will be vitally interested in the arts and would be happiest making his or her living in this area (15c).

If it clings to the Jupiter (first) finger (15d) it is a sign that the person will ultimately obtain influence through his or her career. If these two fingers stand apart from each other, any influence the person manages to achieve will come from outside the career.

The Phalanges

As with the other fingers the three phalanges should all be about equal in size.

If the tip phalange is the longest (15e) the person will be intellectual and interested in spirituality. This person will be proud of his or her intellect and may consider himself or herself to be several steps above other mortals. He or she will also be cautious and prudent. If this tip is extremely long the person will have a negative

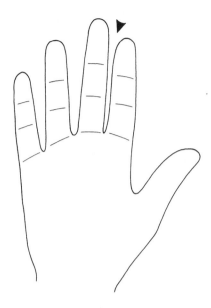

15d. Saturn finger clinging to Jupiter finger

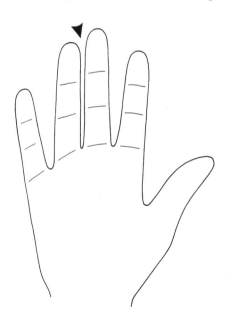

15c. Saturn finger clinging to Apollo finger

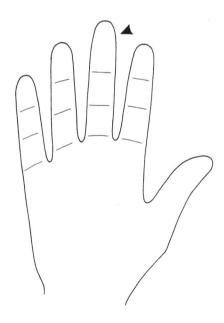

15e. Long tip phalange on Saturn finger

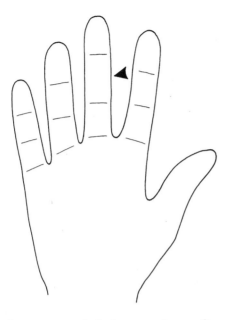

15f. Long second phalange on Saturn finger

approach to everything and be a sad, melancholy individual.

If the middle phalange is the longest (15f) the person will be a good organizer and enjoy performing work that is highly involved or detailed. If the finger is smooth, a long second phalange gives a strong interest in the occult.

If the middle phalange is very short compared to the others (15g), the person will waste a lot of time and not enjoy learning. He or she will be an ignoramus.

A long base phalange (15h) gives an interest in agriculture. You will find this on farmers, keen gardeners, and people who love working on the land.

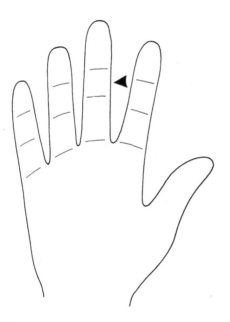

15g. Short second phalange on Saturn finger

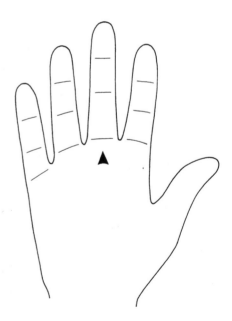

15h. Long third phalange on Saturn finger

CHAPTER SIXTEEN

The Jupiter Finger

THE FIRST FINGER is named after the planet Jupiter, which in turn is named after the king of the gods. It denotes drive, ambition, leadership qualities, and the ego.

Length

The Jupiter finger should reach between half and two-thirds of the way up the tip phalange of the second finger (16a). Ideally, it should be about the same length as the Apollo finger. If it is longer (16b) it gives the person drive and

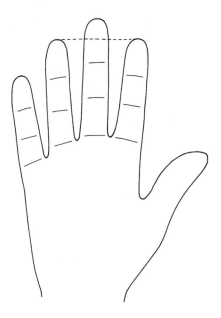

16a. Ideal length of Jupiter finger

ambition. People with a long Jupiter finger are determined to get what they want and keep on working at it until they succeed. The only disadvantage of this is that these people often do not know when to stop, so in extreme cases these people can drive themselves to an early grave. If it is very long compared to the Apollo finger, it can indicate egotism.

If the Jupiter finger is the same length as the Apollo finger it means that the person is moderately ambitious and will work hard for what he or she wants, but also knows when to stop and relax. This person will be realistic in assessing his or her abilities.

It is not always easy to determine the relative lengths of the fingers from the palm side

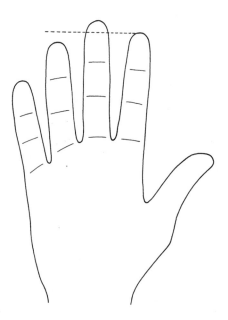

16b. Long Jupiter finger

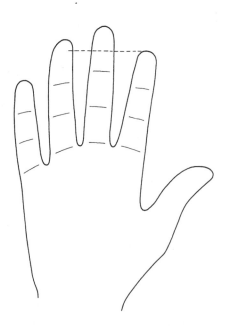

16c. Short Jupiter finger

of the hand. As mentioned earlier, it is often better to assess the relative lengths of the Jupiter and Apollo fingers by turning the hand over and comparing them from the back of the hand.

When the Jupiter finger is shorter than the Apollo finger (16c) it is an indication of lack of confidence early on in life. If this finger is very short it indicates someone who is timid, quiet, and scared of life.

Curved Jupiter Finger

If this finger curves towards the Saturn finger (16d) the person will be self-centered and need constant encouragement. This relates to low self-esteem and lack of confidence.

Phalanges

As with the other fingers the three phalanges should be reasonably equal in length.

If the tip phalange is the longest (16e) the person will have religious or philosophical interests and have a strong sense of dignity. He or she is likely to work in any field involving personal contact with other people. Members of the clergy are usually religious and work with people.

If the middle phalange is longest (16f) the person will be intelligent, practical, and have a positive approach toward his or her goals in life.

The base phalange is more likely to be larger than the others (16g). If this is the case, the person will be interested in philosophy and religion. You could say to this person:

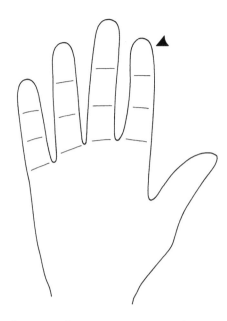

16d. Jupiter finger curving toward Saturn finger

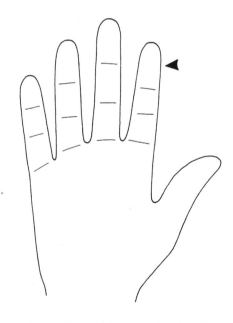

16e. Long first phalange on Jupiter finger

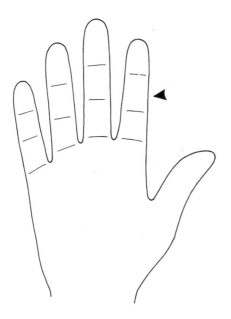

16f. Long second phalange on Jupiter finger

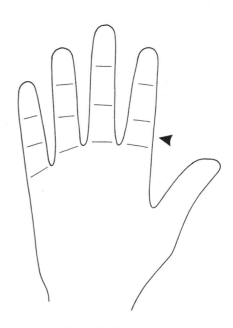

16h. Short third phalange on Jupiter finger

"You will gradually build up a strong faith or philosophy of life. It may or may not be a church type of religion, but whatever it is, it will play an increasingly important role in your life."

If the base phalange is the shortest (16h) the person will be self-effacing and be free of great ambitions. People with a short base phalange are happiest left to themselves, pursuing their own modest dreams.

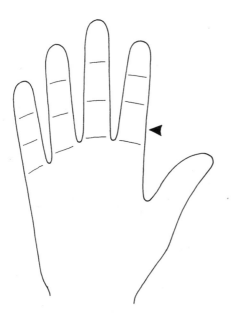

16g. Long third phalange on Jupiter finger

CHAPTER SEVENTEEN

The Mounts

THE MOUNTS ARE small mounds on the surface of the palm (17a). They relate to potential energy and activities the person enjoys doing. Consequently, they are very useful in vocational guidance.

The mounts can be read for both quality and quantity. If the mount is high the person will be energetic and active in the specific areas covered by the mount. He or she will be prepared to put physical energy into the particular qualities the mount indicates. If the mount is wide it shows the potential of the mind. Ideally, we look for high, wide mounts.

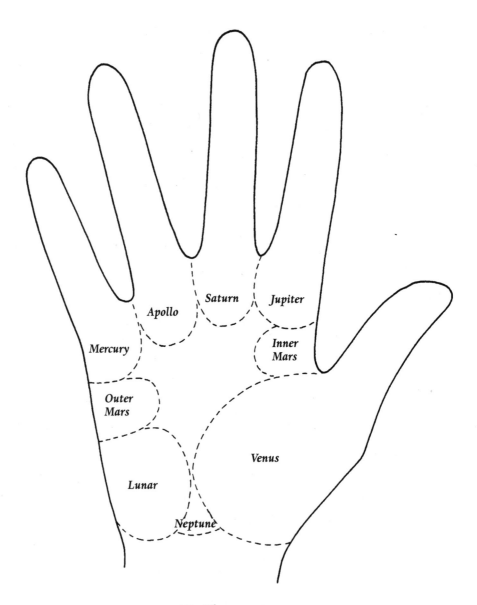

17a. The mounts

First of all, look at all the mounts to find which one predominates in the person's palm. Once you find what appears to be the main mount, press on it and see how firm it is. If the mount is firm, the person will be making use of the knowledge he or she has learned. If the mount is soft, the person will have gained knowledge that is not being utilized.

You will sometimes find hands where all of the mounts seem to be equally strong. Someone with hands like this will have a great deal of drive and ambition and be confident of achieving his or her goals. A palm like this is sometimes known as a "lucky hand."

You will also find hands where it is hard to detect any of the mounts. Someone with hands like this will be lacking in confidence and unsure of his or her ability to succeed. If the hand is firm to the touch, he or she can achieve set goals, but will have to work much harder than someone with strongly visible mounts.

The first four mounts are at the base of the fingers, and the other four are in different parts of the hand. Each of the finger mounts has a central apex, which is a triangular skin ridge pattern similar to fingerprints. You may need a magnifying glass to determine the apex in many mounts. If the apex is sited directly under the middle of the finger, it is a sign that this mount is the most important in the hand. If two or more mounts have centrally sited apexes, each mount is of equal importance.

The Mount of Jupiter

This mount is found at the base of the first finger. If it is well sited and wide as well as high, the person will be a natural leader, someone who can walk in to any situation and immediately take charge. This person will be intelligent, show initiative, and have plenty of self-esteem. He or she will be ambitious and prepared to work hard to achieve his or her aims. A strong Jupiter mount is found on the hands of many people in public life, and also in charismatic religious leaders.

If this mount is high, but spongy rather than firm, the person will be vain and proud. He or she will enjoy showing off and asserting him or herself. He or she could overindulge in a number of areas. Food is most likely to be one of them.

The Mount of Saturn

This mount is found beneath the Saturn finger. If it is well developed the person will have a saturnine approach to life. He or she will be responsible and hard-working, yet tend to be gloomy and solitary. This person will enjoy work that is detailed and can be done on his or her own with little input from others. This person will have good qualities as well, and is usually loved by others. However, he or she will find it difficult to express affection and love in return.

If this mount is wide and spongy to the touch, it is an indication of someone who enjoys wallowing in morbid fantasies.

In practice, this is the mount least likely to be dominant in a hand. Most people have a flat area under the Saturn finger, and this means they do not possess the negative traits associated with the mount.

The Mount of Apollo

This mount is found at the base of the ring, or Apollo, finger. It provides a measure of the person's outlook on success, happiness, and beauty.

A well-developed mount gives enthusiasm, aesthetic tastes, and skill in dealing with others. Someone with this will have good taste and will appreciate beautiful things, whether he or she is capable of creating them or not.

Success is viewed purely in financial terms by many people, and someone with a well developed mount of Apollo will be shrewd in assessing money-making opportunities.

People with a well-developed Apollo mount are adaptable and versatile, able to fit in to any situation and immediately make their presence felt. They are charming and easy to get along with. However, people with a strong Apollo mount have a quick temper as well, but once their annoyance fades these outbursts are quickly forgotten, at least by them!

The main faults of a large mount of Apollo are vanity and a tendency to exaggerate. If this mount is soft and spongy the person is likely to fantasize about great success but do little to achieve it. This person could be a dilettante in creative fields.

If the mount is virtually nonexistent the person will be down-to-earth and practical, but will lack imagination and an appreciation of aesthetic matters.

If the Apollo mount is sited toward the Saturn finger the person is likely to be interested in composing music or writing plays, rather than performing.

If this mount is sited toward the Mercury finger the person is likely to be interested more in performing, producing, or directing. He or she could also be involved in the business side of the arts, and become an impresario or theater manager.

The Mount of Mercury

The mount of Mercury is located under the little finger and is related to the quickness of the mind and the person's ability to think.

People with a well-developed Mercury mount have good brains and are able to express themselves clearly. They are interested in what is going on in the world around them. Challenges are important to them and these could well take the form of competitive sports and games as well as business. They have inventive brains and are able to think quickly on their feet. They make good teachers, debaters, actors, or orators. They are likely to enjoy arguments for the opportunities they provide for quick thinking and repartee.

They are also affectionate and make good partners. They are easy to get along with and are devoted lovers and parents.

If this mount is undeveloped the person is likely to be impractical and insincere. This individual could use his or her gifts of verbal expression to deceive others. An undeveloped mount of Mercury is often found on the hands of confidence tricksters. However, it does not necessarily mean the person is dishonest. An undeveloped mount can create someone with lots of thoughts and grand schemes, but no motivation to achieve them.

It is common for this mount to be sited toward the Apollo finger. This means the person has a cheerful, less serious approach toward life.

If Mercury and Apollo appear to form one large mount the person will be highly creative and interested in examining and exploring a wide range of different subjects.

The Mount of Venus

This mount is at the base of the thumb and is encircled by the life line. This mount forms the thumb's third phalange. It relates to love, affection, passion, vitality, and sympathy.

If this mount is reasonably high and firm the person will be affectionate, sympathetic, and thoroughly enjoy life. He or she will be interested in love and beauty. This person will be happiest inside a good, strong relationship that involves friendship as well as love. He or she will be passionate and have plenty of energy and enthusiasm.

The higher the mount, the greater the passion, so this is an important factor when determining the compatibility of a couple.

Conversely, the lower the mount, the less passion. Many years ago I read the palm of a middle-aged lady who had a Venus mount that was actually inverted. Before I had a chance to open my mouth, she said, "Don't tell me I'm going to get married. I hate men!" Her hand certainly revealed that, but it also showed that she had no love, compassion, or sympathy for anyone.

The breadth of this mount is determined by the life line. If the life line comes well across the palm, the mount of Venus will be large, indicating that the person will be generous in love. He or she will also have plenty of warmth and enthusiasm.

If the life line hugs the thumb, the person will be cautious in every aspect of life and have very little energy or staying power.

The Mounts of Mars

There are two mounts of Mars, one on each side of the palm. They are known as inner and outer Mars.

Inner Mars lies just below the base of the thumb, inside the life line. If the hand is folded slightly you will be able to determine the exact area from the fold of flesh created when the thumb is moved. The degree of firmness in this area indicates the amount of aggression the individual has. It shows whether the person will stand up for him or herself and fight, or run away and hide. It relates to physical courage. If the inner mount is overdeveloped the person will be highly aggressive and argumentative.

Conversely, if it is underdeveloped the person will find it very hard to stick up for him or herself.

Directly across the palm from inner Mars is the mount of outer Mars. This is generally between the head and heart lines. Sometimes, the head line may finish on this mount, but the heart line is always outside. Outer Mars governs self-control and the ability to hang on long after lesser people would have given up. Consequently, this mount is always strong on people who have survived severe adversity. It also relates to moral courage.

If either of the mounts of Mars are strong, the person will be generous and prepared to stand up and defend his or her friends. He or she will also have great energy and staying power. Strong mounts of Mars are a wonderful asset to people engaged in competitive sports as it gives them great energy, determination, persistence, and aggression.

The area between the two mounts of Mars is called the plain of Mars. This area should be firm to the touch. If the two mounts of Mars are well developed it may appear to be sunken or hollow. You can test the firmness by pressing your thumb on the plain with your fingers supporting the back of the hand. As the heart, head, and destiny lines all cross this area it is important that it be strong, as then the person can make best use of the qualities of these lines. If the plain of Mars is weak or spongy to the touch the person will make mistakes in choosing friends, and will allow him or herself to be influenced by them, even while knowing their suggestions are wrong. You will find this in the hands of many teenagers, but fortunately, with maturity this area usually firms.

The Mount of Luna

The mount of Luna lies at the base of the hand on the side of the little finger, directly opposite the thumb. This mount rules the creative subconscious and governs imagination and creativity. It reveals the person's emotional nature.

Ideally, this mount should be firm to the touch and have a clear apex on it. The apex is a skin ridge pattern that we will cover in the chapter on dermatoglyphics. When the apex is well developed the individual will have an active imagination and be interested in creative pursuits. If it is the predominant mount on the hand the person will have a tendency to daydream and lack the necessary drive to achieve his or her grand dreams. If this is the dominant mount on a man's hand he is usually effeminate. A woman is inclined to be superficial and frivolous if Luna is the main mount in her hand.

The Mount of Neptune

This mount is found at the base of the hand by the wrist, between the Luna and Venus mounts. When firm it creates a level surface on the palm where the Luna, Venus, and Neptune mounts meet.

This mount gives ability at public speaking, and is an indication of someone who can think quickly on his or her feet. It is a great asset for anyone who performs for the public.

If the mount is undeveloped the person will have difficulties in expressing his or her innermost feelings.

Displaced Mounts

Frequently, you will find the mounts are not exactly where you would expect to find them. When they are displaced in this way the meanings change slightly. The center of each mount is found by looking for the apex or tri-radius. This is where the skin ridge pattern forms a small triangle with one angle pointing toward the finger it is below and the other two angles indicating the mounts on either side.

If the Jupiter mount is displaced toward the edge of the palm the person will be egotistical. If it is displaced toward the thumb the person will be extremely aware of his or her family background and this will influence every action. If it is displaced toward Saturn he or she will be self-conscious, but will gain some of the Saturn qualities of thoughtfulness and wisdom.

If Saturn is displaced toward Jupiter the individual will gain some of Jupiter's qualities of optimism and self-confidence. Displaced toward Apollo, the more serious characteristics of Saturn are lost in favor of a more positive outlook on life, though the person will still need quite a bit of time on his or her own.

When the mount of Apollo is displaced toward Saturn the person will relate well to very young people and would be highly suited to a career dealing with children. If Apollo is displaced toward Mercury the person will have an affinity with all living things, particularly animals.

If Mercury is displaced toward Apollo the individual will refuse to take anything seriously and will have a lighthearted approach to life. It is not found often, but when Mercury is displaced toward the edge of the palm the person will show great courage in the face of danger.

CHAPTER EIGHTEEN

Palm Patterns

DERMATOGLYPHICS IS A long word to describe the skin ridge patterns on the palm. The most commonly known dermatoglyphics are our fingerprints, and these come in three main patterns: loops, whorls, and arches (18a, b, c).

Loops are found more frequently than the others in the Western world. People with loops on every finger are adaptable and able to fit in to almost any situation. They work well as part of a team.

Whorls indicate an individualist. It is rare to find someone with whorls on every finger. The

18a. Loop, fingerprint pattern

18b. Whorl fingerprint pattern

18c. Arch fingerprint pattern

18d. Tri-radii

presence of a whorl gives originality to whatever quality the finger represents. For instance, someone with a whorl on the Apollo finger would be highly original and creative.

Arches belong to the plodders of this world. Someone with arches on every finger would be practical, reliable, and conscientious.

A variation of the arch is the tented arch, which is a high arch similar to the loop. Someone with tented arches will get very enthusiastic about all sorts of things, but the interest may not last long.

Tri-Radii

Tri-radii are the small triangles found at the top of each finger mount (18d). In addition to these four, you will frequently find one on the top of the mount of Luna and sometimes on the mount of Neptune. A tri-radius here is a strong indicator of psychic potential.

Loop Patterns

There are thirteen loops that can be found on the palm (18e). Do not be alarmed if you fail to find any on your hands, as not everyone has them. You will usually find one or two loops on the average hand. I find it intriguing that palmists in past centuries paid no attention to them as they are not mentioned in old books on palmistry. Research into the subject is still very recent, and this is an area where you can make original contributions through your own observation and study. However, it would pay to become familiar with hand shapes and lines before becoming overly involved in this aspect of palmistry.

The Loop of Humor

This loop is located between the Mercury and Apollo fingers and gives the person a slightly offbeat sense of humor (18e-1). The larger the loop, the greater the sense of the ridiculous. This loop is the one most likely to be found on a hand. The absence of this loop does not mean that the person has no sense of humor. Someone with it always has a slightly "different" sense of humor.

The Loop of Ego

This loop is occasionally mistaken for the loop of humor as it also starts between the Mercury and Apollo fingers (18e-2). It always slants across on to the mount of Apollo, however. People with this loop have a strong sense of their own self-importance, but are extremely sensitive with it. Consequently, their egos can be damaged very easily.

The Loop of Common Sense

This loop is found between the Apollo and Saturn fingers (18e-3) and belongs to people who keep their feet on the ground and think before acting. People with this loop also have a strong sense of responsibility and a desire to help others. It is this latter meaning that has

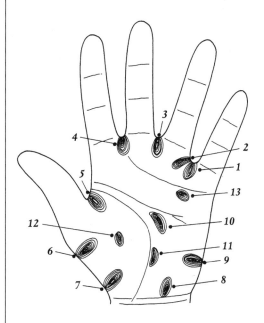

18e. Loops in the palm

led to this formation being sometimes known as the "loop of good intent."

The Rajah Loop

The rajah loop is found between the Jupiter and Saturn fingers (18e-4) and in traditional Indian palmistry is supposed to indicate that people with it have royal blood in their veins. Several of the people I have seen with this formation are descended from royalty, but I have also found it on the palms of people who have no knowledge of their family history. Whether the royal connection is valid or not, you will always find that people with this loop have a special aura or charisma about them that draws other people to them.

The Loop of Courage

This loop lies directly between the base of the thumb and the start of the life line, on the mount of Mars (18e-5). People with the loop of courage do not show fear, no matter how daunting the situation may be. They value courage and are prepared to stand up valiantly for their beliefs. They are also interested in hearing about other people's courageous exploits and try to live up to these examples in their own lives.

The Loop of Response

The loop of response lies on the mount of Venus between the base of the thumb and the wrist (18e-6). People with this marking have a remarkable ability to respond to the feelings of whichever group they happen to be in. If the group is serious, they will be serious. If everyone is relaxing and having a good time, they will automatically do the same.

They also show a marked response to their environment. If their surroundings are dull and dingy they feel apathetic and depressed. If the environment is pleasant and comfortable they blossom and feel full of the joys of life. The response felt by people like this is so marked that if they were confined in prison, for example, they would be likely to suffer mental problems.

People with a loop of response also thoroughly enjoy brass music, and would much rather listen to a band recital than an orchestral concert.

The Loop of Music

This loop commences at the wrist and lies on the mount of Venus (18e-7). It gives a great love of music. If the person also has an angle of pitch on his palm he or she will have a musical talent that should be developed. This could be singing, playing an instrument, or even composing.

The Loop of Inspiration

The loop of inspiration is found at the base of the palm in the area between the Venus and Luna mounts (18e-8). People with this loop have the capacity to be really inspired by something that affects them. This is usually music, literature, or humanitarian deeds, but can be almost anything that these people find uplifting and inspiring. This loop is very rare and people who possess it have the power to change our world for the better. This loop can make the difference between someone being a competent musician and a great composer. It is interesting to speculate how many great artists of the past had a loop of inspiration on their hands.

The Ulnar Loop

This loop is sometimes referred to as the "loop of nature" as people with it have an uncanny awareness of all the workings of nature. A good dowser or someone with "green fingers" is likely to have an ulnar loop.

The ulnar loop is found rising from the edge of the palm on to the mount of Luna (18e-9). Ideally, it should be at least halfway along the Luna mount toward the wrist, as then the person can use it to gain access to his or her creative subconscious mind.

This loop is always an indication of something a little bit different in the workings of the person's mind and is most frequently found on the hands of Down's syndrome people. It is found on about 8 percent of normal hands, but on some 90 percent of the hands of Down's syndrome people. However, like the simian crease, its presence does not indicate that there is anything mentally wrong with the person. It is interesting that Down's syndrome people often have a great love of nature.

The Loop of Memory

This loop is found near the center of the palm. It usually starts near the mount of Jupiter and heads across the palm toward the mount of Luna, often parallel to the head line (18e-10).

The loop of memory always gives its owner an extremely good memory. A friend of mine with this loop has an almost photographic memory for anything he has ever read, yet makes his living as a storeman in a warehouse. He loves information for its own sake and has no desire to use this talent to further his own career.

The Humanitarian Loop

The humanitarian loop is very rare. It is found in the center of the palm, parallel to the destiny line and heading towards the wrist (18e-11).

People with this loop are total idealists and find it hard to live in our material world. They try to change the world, and consequently have more than their share of disappointments and disillusion. On a strong hand this loop can be an asset, giving the person scope to develop his or her humanitarian ideals.

Loop of Stringed Music

This is an oval loop occasionally found in the center of the Venus mount (18e-12). It gives an appreciation of music, similar to the loop of music, but with a special empathy toward music played on stringed instruments. Someone with this loop will prefer chamber music or an orchestral concert to a band recital.

Loop of Recall

The loop of recall is a small loop found between the heart and head lines (18e-13). Someone with this loop has a retentive memory and the ability to recall information easily. If the head line runs over this loop this ability is increased. If the person also possesses a loop of memory, he or she will have a strong intellect and possess an almost photographic memory.

CHAPTER NINETEEN

The Quadrangle and Great Triangle

THE SPACE BETWEEN the heart and head lines is called the quadrangle. Ideally, in an average size hand, the two lines should be about half an inch apart throughout most of the quadrangle, becoming wider at each end (19a). On larger hands the two lines should be correspondingly further apart. Someone with this formation will be well balanced, even tempered, and have a good sense of humor. He or she will be extremely easy to get along with, being obliging, helpful, and willing to lend a helping hand when necessary.

Narrow Quadrangle

When the heart and head lines are very close together for most of their length the person will lack humor and imagination. He or she will be narrow-minded and miserly (19b).

Wide Quadrangle

If the heart and head lines are well apart (19c) the person will be an independent thinker in some areas, but be extremely gullible in others. He or she will be easily influenced by others and be overly anxious to please. This person will also be careless and unconventional. The

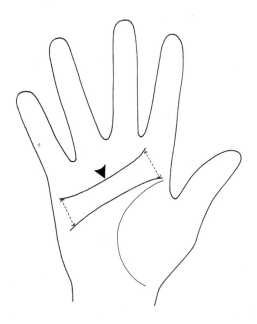

19a. Ideal quadrangle

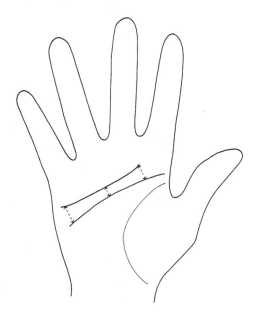

19b. Narrow quadrangle

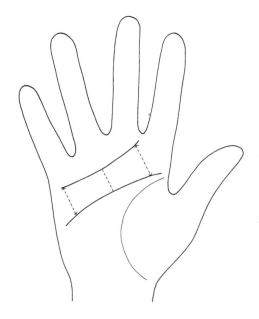

19c. Wide quadrangle

wider the quadrangle is the more outgoing and extroverted the person will be.

Irregular Quadrangle

The quadrangle is said to be irregular if it is wider at one end than the other (19d). Someone with this formation is likely to be full of the joys of life at one moment and then be in the depths of despair a moment later. In Indian palmistry it is believed that if the wider portion is on the side of the little finger the person will not repay his debts. This has not been my experience. If the wider portion is at the thumb side the Indians believe he or she will return any money borrowed.

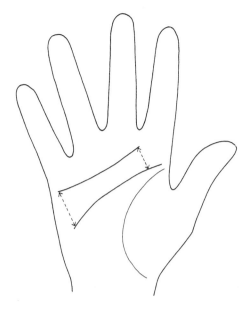

19d. Irregular quadrangle

Waisted Quadrangle

If the quadrangle is much wider at each end than the middle (19e), the person is likely to be unsettled and lack confidence between the ages of thirty-five and forty-nine.

Lines in the Quadrangle

Ideally, there should be as few lines as possible inside the quadrangle except for those, such as the destiny line, that are following their natural course. In this area the person is reaping the rewards of everything he or she has done up until the age of thirty-five. In the quadrangle the person is carrying on, consolidating, or

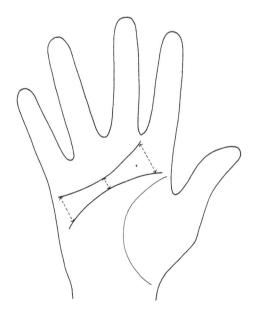

19e. Quadrangle wider at each end (waisted)

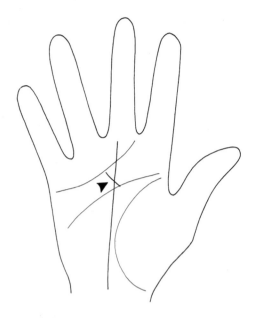

19f. Cross on destiny line inside quadrangle

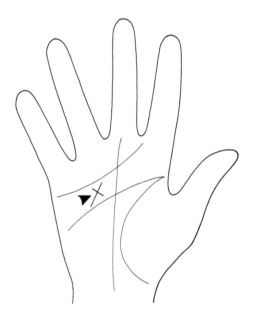

**19g. Unattached cross in
quadrangle (mystic cross)**

rebuilding his or her life in the middle years. Any extra lines in the quadrangle are likely to impede progress at this stage.

As you already know, the destiny line enters the quadrangle at the age of thirty-five and leaves it again at forty-nine. If the destiny line ends inside the quadrangle it shows that the person has become set in his or her ways. Someone like this is no longer prepared to work hard to better him or herself, but will instead take life as it comes.

If the destiny line appears to break up into a series of small lines that finally disappear it is a sign of failure, all the more tragic as the person no longer has the energy to try and become successful again.

You will frequently find a large cross inside the quadrangle. One branch of the cross is formed by the destiny line and the other line crosses it diagonally (19f). This is an indication of ultimate success, but the person will experience a large number of setbacks along the way. It can be very frustrating to have this cross, particularly if the person is lacking in patience.

You will occasionally find another well-defined cross inside the quadrangle that is not attached to any major line (19g). This is called the mystic cross and gives a strong interest in psychic matters.

The Great Triangle

The great triangle is formed by the life line, head line, and generally the destiny line (19h). Sometimes the third side of the triangle is created by the hepatica, or health line.

Most people have a great triangle on their palms, and it is of great importance only when it suddenly seems to leap out of the palm and become the most obvious feature at a casual glance. When the triangle is like this it is an indication that the person is about to achieve great success of some sort. Something he or she has been working towards for some time is about to come to fruition.

At all times a good-sized, evenly formed triangle is an indication of broadmindedness and generosity. The larger the triangle is, the better. The smaller the triangle is, the more narrow and selfish will be the outlook of its owner.

In Indian palmistry it is believed that if all three corners of the triangle are closed the person will be good at saving money.

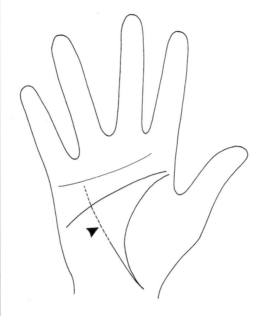

19h. The great triangle

CHAPTER TWENTY

Degrees of the Palm

ONCE YOU BECOME practiced at reading palms you will be able to recognize the different degrees, or qualities, at a glance (20a). These degrees provide excellent information about a person's character, and you will find knowledge of them very useful in daily life. For instance, if you happen to notice that someone you work with has a pronounced degree of inferiority you can then take steps to boost their self-esteem.

You have already learned this information in previous chapters, but thinking about it in

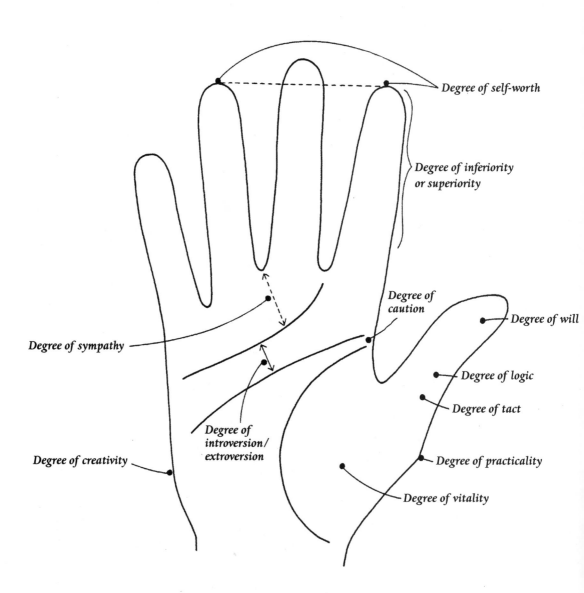

20a. Degrees of the palm

terms of "degrees" provides a different way of looking at it. Regarding different factors as degrees allows you to make quick assessments that can be very helpful in reading palms.

Degree of Sympathy

This is determined by how far down the palm the heart line is. The further away from the fingers it is, the more sympathetic and understanding the person will be. If the heart line hugs close to the fingers the person will be unfeeling, unsympathetic, and critical.

Degree of Extroversion

The degree of extroversion is determined by the distance between the heart and head lines, in the quadrangle. If the heart and head lines are close together the person will be basically introverted. The wider the space becomes, the more outgoing and extroverted the person will be.

Degree of Vitality

The degree of vitality is determined by the breadth, height, and firmness of the mount of Venus. If the life line is clearly marked and encircles a firm Venus in a wide arc reaching well across the hand, the person will have plenty of energy and staying power. Conversely, if the life line is weak and hugs closely to the thumb, the person will have little energy and appear to be only half alive.

If the mount of Venus is full, but flabby, the person will have great ideas but will never get around to doing any of them. When things go wrong, this individual will always blame others rather than him or herself.

Degree of Creativity

The degree of creativity is measured by the size of the curve on the percussion (little finger) side of the palm. As this curve is usually created by a good-sized mount of Luna, which governs the creative subconscious, a bulge on this side of the palm is an indication of creative ability. We have to look at other parts of the hand to determine how the creativity is put into use.

Degree of Caution

The degree of caution is measured by seeing if the head and life lines are joined at the start. If they are joined, the person will be basically cautious. If separated, he or she will be more independent. This person can also be impulsive and jump into new activities without thinking first. The more widely separated these lines are, the more extreme the impulsiveness.

Degree of Logic

The degree of logic is determined by the size of the second phalange on the thumb. If it is longer than the first phalange, the person will like to think things out carefully before acting. If the second phalange is shorter than the nail phalange, he or she will act first and think later.

Degree of Will

Like logic, this is also measured in the thumb. If the tip phalange is longer than the second phalange the person will act first and think later, but will also have a great drive to succeed. This person will make many mistakes along the way, but will pick him or herself up again each time and continue.

If the tip section is shorter than the second section the person will be lacking in will power. He or she may be full of wonderful ideas, but they usually stay as ideas as there is a lack of motivation and incentive to put them into practice.

Degree of Tact

The degree of tact is shown by the second phalange of the thumb. If this phalange bows inward on both sides, creating a waisted appearance, the person will be naturally tactful and diplomatic. If the second phalange is thick and oblong in appearance, the person will be lacking in tact.

Degree of Practicality

The degree of practicality the person possesses is found by looking at the size of the angle created by the outside of the thumb where it joins the palm. This is the angle of practicality. Someone with a large bump at this point will be good with his or her hands. In fact, these hands will virtually be able to think for themselves. I always choose a plumber, builder, TV repairman, or any other tradesperson by the size of his or her degree of practicality.

Degree of Self-Worth

The degree of self-worth is measured by the length of the Jupiter finger compared with the Apollo finger. If these fingers are equal in length the person has a good self-image and relates well in the world. If the Jupiter finger is shorter than the Apollo finger the person lacked confidence early on in life and is not totally sure of his or her worth. The shorter the finger is in comparison with the Apollo finger, the greater the feelings of inferiority the person will carry around.

If the Jupiter finger is longer than the Apollo finger the person will have plenty of confidence and ambition. The longer the Jupiter finger is, however, the greater the feelings of superiority he or she has over the rest of humanity.

CHAPTER
TWENTY-ONE

Other Factors
in the Hand

So FAR WE have looked at the shape of the hand, the four main lines, and the fingers and thumb. We have not yet looked at psychic abilities, money, health, travel, romance, and children. In fact, these are usually the very items our clients want covered in the greatest detail!

Psychic Ability

I believe that we all have this talent, but not everybody chooses to do anything with it. People with latent psychic abilities will possess at the very least a line of intuition.

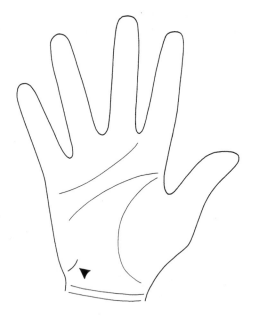

21a. Line of intuition

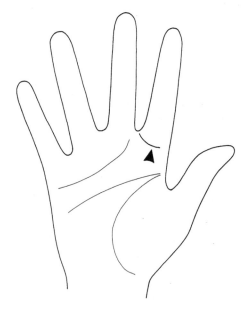

21b. Ring of Solomon

This is a fine line running from the outside of the palm, close to the wrist, in toward the middle of the palm (21a). It is usually a very short, fine line, though you will sometimes find people with long lines of intuition. Long lines are very helpful, as we can determine how the individual can best use his or her psychic abilities. If it veers toward the head line, the person would make a very natural psychic, or spiritual, healer. If it heads toward the destiny line the person would be naturally good at telepathy, clairvoyance, or precognition. This is not to say that someone with a line of intuition heading toward the head line would not make a good clairvoyant. This person certainly could be, but his or her talents would more naturally gravitate toward healing.

Some people have two fine lines of intuition running parallel to each other. These people can get premonitions in their dreams. Whenever I see this I suggest the person keep a dream diary by their bed and record their dreams as soon as they wake up.

People with intuition lines are sensitive, caring, and highly attuned to other people's feelings. They are invariably interested in psychic matters and are natural healers.

Normally, the intuition lines show on both hands. People with an intuition line in the minor hand only are aware of their capabilities in this area but are afraid to trust or develop this natural talent.

As well as the lines of intuition, we look for what is called the ring of Solomon. This is a curve running around the mount of Jupiter

(21b). Do not confuse this with a straight line that is often found in the same position known as a sympathy line (21c). People with this line have a naturally sympathetic, understanding outlook. The ring of Solomon is curved, and it gives the person an interest in the psychic world.

The presence of a mystic cross (19g) in the quadrangle is also a sign of interest in psychic matters. It is a small cross that is self-contained and does not overlap any other line.

People with a ring of Solomon, line of intuition, and mystic cross have a definite head start over people without them as far as developing their psychic abilities are concerned. People who do not have these markings, however, quickly develop them if they become interested in psychic matters.

Money

Everybody becomes interested when you start talking about money on their palm! Inherited money is shown by a fine curving line beside the base of the Apollo finger on the side of the Mercury finger (21d). This line simply means that the person will come into money at some stage in their life. It gives no clue as to when.

Earned money is shown by a triangle formed on two sides by the crossing of the head and destiny lines (21e). On the percussion (edge of the hand opposite the thumb) side of this conjunction you will find a small triangle. Ideally, it should be a completely closed triangle as this means the person can

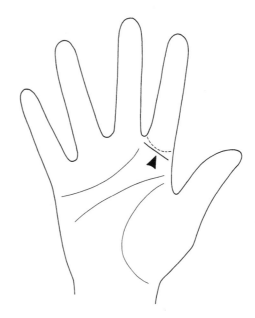

21c. Sympathy line

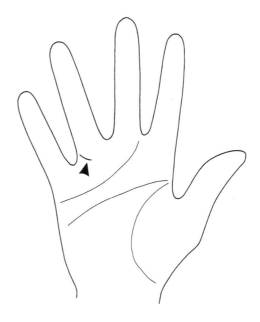

21d. Inherited money

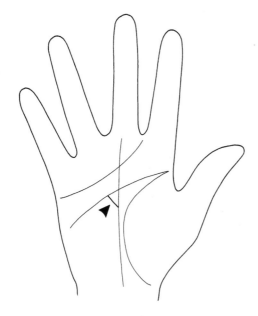

21e. Money triangle

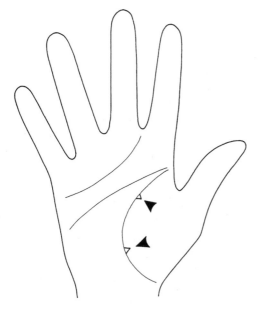

21f. Money that is won

hang on to some of the money once he or she has it. If it is partially open, it means that although money comes in, most manages to escape again as well. When there is no third side to the triangle, the money comes in and goes straight out again. The larger the triangle, the greater the person's potential. However, do not assume that someone will become a millionaire because he or she has a large triangle. You have to look at other factors, particularly motivation, to see if this person will work hard to get it. The triangle indicates earned money, after all.

How easily the money is earned can often be discovered by the presence of a fine line running from the life line to one of the finger mounts. If the line ends on the Jupiter mount the person will ultimately achieve great success in their career. This indicates honors and recognition, as well as money. If it ends on the Saturn mount it will come through plain hard work. If it ends on the Apollo mount it is an indication of someone who is lucky in winning money. Finally, if the line ends on the mount of Mercury it shows the money will be earned in the business or scientific world.

Lottery wins are shown by small triangles on the inside of the life line (21f). The life line provides one of the sides of this triangle, and the placement of the triangle shows when the money will be won. Very few people have these, as most of us have to work hard for our money. Many years ago I read the palm of a young man who had three of these triangles. I commented with some amazement on this, and found he had already won one large lottery and had two more to go!

Travel

Travel lines are shown as fine lines on the percussion side of the palm (21g). You start reading these from near the wrist and they can appear all the way down to where the heart line begins.

Some people have no travel lines at all. This does not mean that they never travel; rather, it shows that they have no interest in travel. Other people will have what seem to be dozens of fine lines. Again this does not mean that they will be traveling all the time. It shows that they daydream and think about travel a great deal, and if the opportunity arose, they would be off somewhere at the drop of a hat.

These people usually manage to find some way of achieving this aim. However, it is not rare to find people with many of these lines who have not traveled. Circumstances have conspired to prevent these people from widening their horizons and traveling. This could be family obligations, or lack of money, confidence, or motivation.

A large number of people fit in the middle, with a reasonable number of clear, well-defined travel lines. These lines indicate important trips. Someone who made her living as an airline hostess would not have every single trip shown on her hand, as she is simply doing her job and travel is a necessary part of it. These trips are

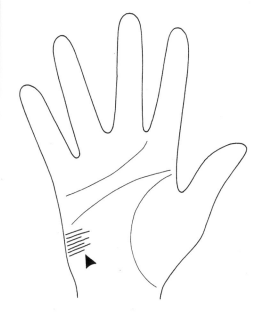

21g. Travel (restlessness) lines

not important. She is likely to have a number of travel lines on her hand though, as she is certain to have an interest in travel to choose that particular career. These lines will indicate the important travel in her life. Usually, the first overseas trip someone does is marked very clearly. After that, only the important trips are shown.

The correct name for these lines are restlessness lines. People with them always need something to look forward to. They do not enjoy routine and love change and variety. Most people daydream and fantasize about travel to exotic locations, and these are revealed by many very fine travel lines.

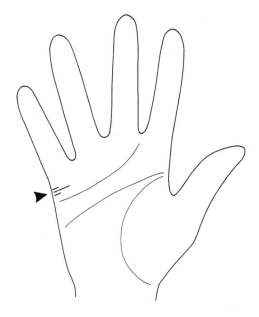

21h. Relationship lines

Romance

Along with the life line, many people are aware of the fine lines on the percussion side of the palm between the base of the little finger and the heart line (21h). These lines are commonly referred to as marriage lines, which is not correct. They are actually relationship lines and show the number of important relationships in a person's life. You may be surprised to hear that I have read the palms of many people who are married but have no relationship lines on their hands. This shows that the marriage is convenient and comfortable, but not of great account to these people. I have never seen this situation on a woman's hand, but have seen it a number of times on the hands of men.

Most people have one, two, three, or maybe four of these relationship lines. They are read in order from the heart line down toward the Mercury finger. For a relationship to be permanent, which often, but not necessarily, means marriage, the line has to come up and over the side of the hand finishing on the palm. If the line does not come over the top it means the relationship does not last.

One difficult aspect in reading these lines is that if a relationship is strong, but finishes and then starts again, it will be shown on the hand as two lines, even though it was the same person both times.

To complicate things still further, it indicates a potential, not necessarily the actuality.

Children

In the past it was possible to go to a palmist, preferably a Gypsy, to find out how many children you were going to have. The children lines show a woman's potential, rather than the actual number of children she will have. Nowadays, we have control over this and it is possible to see people with large potentials who choose not to have any children. A hundred years ago that would not have been so easy to arrange!

The children lines are fine lines directly under the Mercury finger, usually attached to a relationship line, heading down toward the finger (21i). You may need a magnifying glass to accurately count them. Nowadays, the strong, well-marked lines show the number of children the person will probably have, though this is not terribly accurate. The strong lines are an accurate indicator of the number of children the person will be close to, and these may include nephews and nieces, for instance.

On a man's hand you will see only the children he will be close to. Every so often you will find a man with, say, three children, but only two strong lines. This does not necessarily mean that he is not the father of one of the children. It shows that he is very close to two of them, and may not have much of a relationship with the third.

These lines can appear very quickly. A close friend of mine could not have children of her own. She managed to adopt a baby, and within three weeks of doing this had a very proud line representing her new baby.

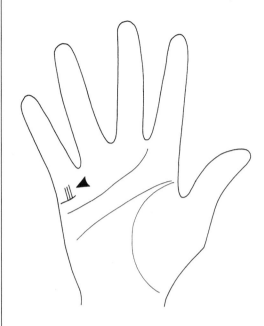

21i. Children lines

CHAPTER
TWENTY-TWO

Romance and Compatibility

SOME PEOPLE SEEM to be natural romantics, while others appear to be totally lacking in this area. To determine how romantic someone is we look first at the height and quality of the mount of Venus. The higher this is, the more romantic the person will be, providing it is reasonably firm. If the mount is high and spongy, the person will be sensual and interested primarily in satisfying his or her own needs. Venus shows the amount of physical energy and stamina we possess, and also reveals the degree of sexuality. Someone with a firm, high mount

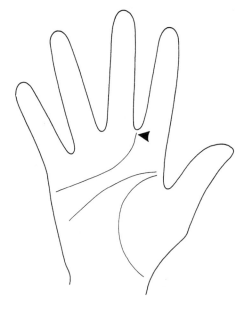

22a. Partner A

will have a strong sexual drive which would be best satisfied in a relationship with someone else with a similar mount of Venus.

Someone with a creative, curving head line will be more romantic than someone with a straight, practical, down-to-earth line. Again, though, we want balance. People with head lines that swoop right down into the mount of Luna are likely to live in a world of daydreams and fantasies. These people will be romantic, and in love with the idea of being in love. Unless they have some strong character traits shown elsewhere on their hands, they will always be disappointed with the realities of life and will retreat into a fantasy world where everything is perfect.

Compatibility

Compatibility is a fascinating area. I believe that almost any relationship can work as long as there is love and good will on both sides. However, some relationships seem to involve an inordinate amount of work to remain viable, and it is generally just one person in the relationship doing all the work!

Hand Shapes

First of all, look at the hand shapes as this reveals the basic temperaments of the people involved. It is a positive sign if both people have the same types of hands. Fire and fire go well together, for instance, as both partners have similar temperaments.

It is not quite as easy if the hand shapes are different. Fire and earth do not relate well, as fire scorches earth. Fire and air get on famously, as air fans and stimulates fire. Fire and water do not get on, as water puts out the fire. Earth and air get on well, as air allows living things to grow and flourish on earth. Earth and water also get on, as water enables life to exist on earth. Air and water are both necessary for survival, but do little for each other. A relationship between these two would be placid and unexciting.

Heart Lines

Once you have determined the hand shapes, look at the ending positions of the heart lines.

The heart lines should be reasonably similar on both parties' hands and should end at the same place. Bear in mind that if one partner has a chained heart line he or she will have had disappointments in love, and will want to be very sure of any new relationship this time before giving totally of him or herself.

Ideally, the heart lines should end between the Jupiter and Saturn fingers as this shows that both people have realistic expectations and are not expecting perfection. If both people have heart lines ending on the mount of Jupiter they will be overly idealistic and will have their share of disappointments. This is more difficult if just one partner has a heart line ending on Jupiter, as this person will be constantly disappointed at what he or she sees as the partner's imperfections. If one person's heart line ends on the Saturn mount, he or she will be selfish and think only of his or her own needs. It is hard to imagine a happy relationship when both partners have heart lines ending on Saturn.

If one person has a mental heart line and the other a physical, you still need to determine if they both finish in a similar place (22a, 22b). For instance, the physical heart line may end between the Jupiter and Saturn fingers, and the mental heart line may end at a spot directly in line from between the Jupiter and Saturn fingers. This still indicates compatibility, but the mental heart line denotes a more impersonal love and difficulty in expressing innermost thoughts, whilst the partner with the physical heart line is more direct and pos-

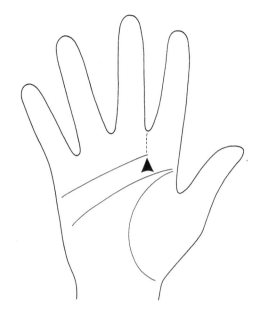

22b. Partner B

sessive. The partner with the mental heart line would want flowers, small gifts, and constant reassurance from the other that he or she is loved. This person would also tend to be a little detached at times. A number of compromises would have to be made by both partners in this relationship.

Thumbs

After you have assessed the shape of the hands and the quality of the heart lines, it is time to look at the thumbs. For compatibility, they should be similar. Imagine the relationship if one person had a strong, thick, stubborn thumb and the other a small, flexible thumb. The second person would be constantly dominated by the other. If both partners have strong, stubborn thumbs they are going to have to learn to compromise. They will have some interesting learning experiences along the way, but ultimately will manage to adjust. If both partners have highly flexible thumbs they will get along very well, as both will be adaptable and want to please. However, they would most likely have difficulties in making important decisions.

Mount of Venus

Finally, check the mount of Venus again. As mentioned earlier, both partners should have Venus mounts of about the same size and height. Imagine the difficulties a couple would have if one partner had a high, firm mount, denoting a strong sex drive, and the other partner had a low, almost inverted mount, indicating that sex is unappealing and preferably a very occasional event. If a couple have mounts of Venus of similar height and degree of firmness, they are likely to be sexually compatible.

CHAPTER
TWENTY-THREE

Talents and Careers

ONE OF THE THINGS that gives me the greatest pleasure in palm reading is to help someone find the right career. It is sad to read the palms of people who have been unhappy in their working lives for twenty or thirty years, but have no idea what they should be doing. A palmist cannot say, "You will be working as a clerk in an insurance company," but can tell the person the type of work he or she would be happiest in. Naturally, if the person enjoys the work he or she is going to be successful at it as well. There are few things more satisfying

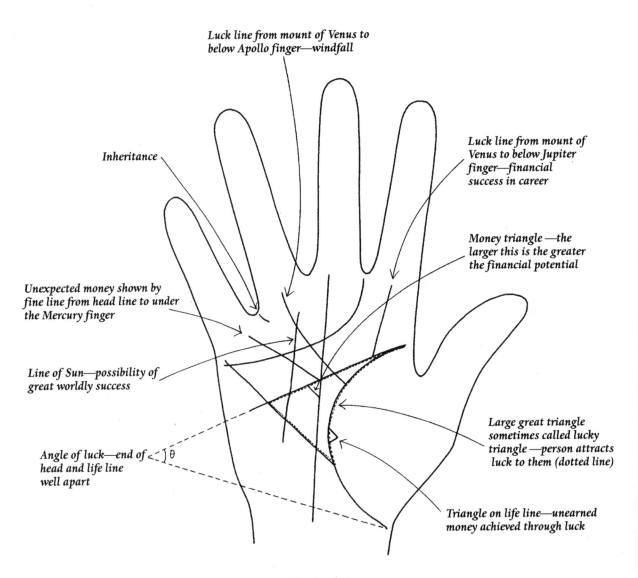

Luck line from mount of Venus to below Apollo finger—windfall

Luck line from mount of Venus to below Jupiter finger—financial success in career

Inheritance

Money triangle —the larger this is the greater the financial potential

Unexpected money shown by fine line from head line to under the Mercury finger

Line of Sun—possibility of great worldly success

Large great triangle sometimes called lucky triangle —person attracts luck to them (dotted line)

Angle of luck—end of head and life line well apart

Triangle on life line—unearned money achieved through luck

23a. Lucky person

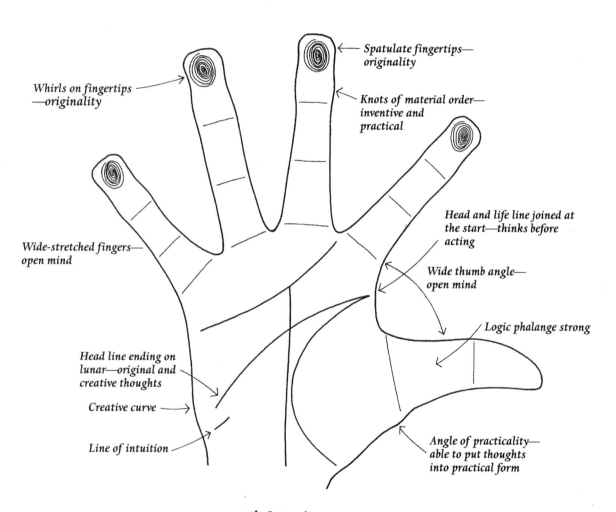

Whirls on fingertips
—originality

Spatulate fingertips—
originality

Knots of material order—
inventive and
practical

Wide-stretched fingers—
open mind

Head and life line joined at
the start—thinks before
acting

Wide thumb angle—
open mind

Logic phalange strong

Head line ending on
lunar—original and
creative thoughts

Creative curve

Line of intuition

Angle of practicality—
able to put thoughts
into practical form

23b. Inventive person

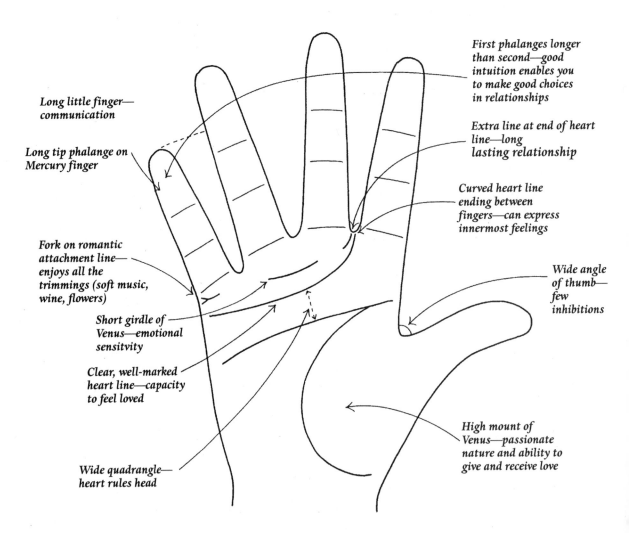

First phalanges longer than second—good intuition enables you to make good choices in relationships

Extra line at end of heart line—long lasting relationship

Long little finger—communication

Curved heart line ending between fingers—can express innermost feelings

Long tip phalange on Mercury finger

Fork on romantic attachment line—enjoys all the trimmings (soft music, wine, flowers)

Wide angle of thumb—few inhibitions

Short girdle of Venus—emotional sensitvity

Clear, well-marked heart line—capacity to feel loved

High mount of Venus—passionate nature and ability to give and receive love

Wide quadrangle—heart rules head

23c. Romantic person

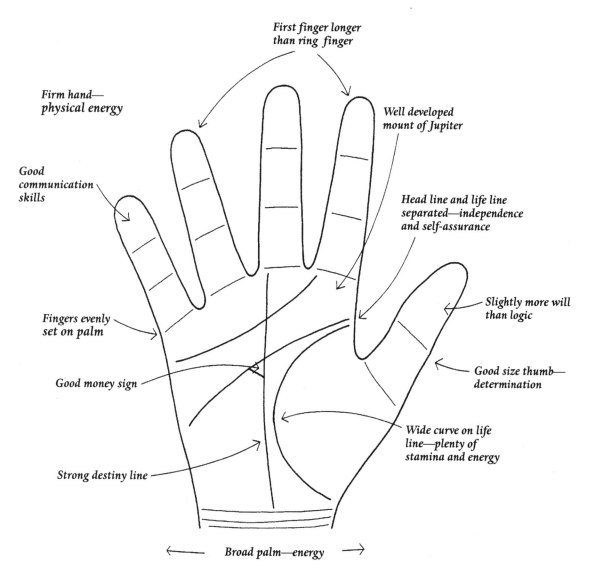

First finger longer
than ring finger

Firm hand—
physical energy

Well developed
mount of Jupiter

Good
communication
skills

Head line and life line
separated—independence
and self-assurance

Slightly more will
than logic

Fingers evenly
set on palm

Good money sign

Good size thumb—
determination

Strong destiny line

Wide curve on life
line—plenty of
stamina and energy

Broad palm—energy

It is not necessary for all of these qualities to be present

23d. Ambitious person

than to read the hands of a teenager who has no idea what career to pursue, and then to follow this person's later progress after helping him or her find the right niche.

Hand Shapes

The shape of the hand gives us the first clue. Someone with a square palm needs to be in a practical field. If this person has a good destiny line he or she would do well in management or business. If the palm is oblong the person will be imaginative and will need opportunities to utilize his or her thoughts and ideas.

Someone with an air hand will be happy in a field involving communication with others. Radio or television announcing, teaching, and sales are all careers that come to mind. This person will be reliable, conscientious, and use his or her analytical brain well.

Someone with a fire hand is likely to be more outgoing than an air hand colleague. The person with a fire hand will use intuition to make quick decisions. He or she will need change, variety, and some way to express him or herself. This person would be good at sales or any other career where he or she is left to get on with it.

If your client has an earth hand he or she will enjoy repetitive tasks and relish practical work. This person will be reliable, honest, and have hands that can think for themselves. He or she would be happy as a carpenter, plumber, mechanic, or in any other field that used both head and hands.

Someone with a water hand will need pleasant surroundings and work that provides aesthetic pleasure. If this person is creative, he or she will be able to develop this talent, but may need constant encouragement from family and friends to keep working. Suitable careers would include interior design, fashion, and theater.

The Mounts

The mounts reveal what the person enjoys doing, so are extremely helpful in vocational analysis.

If Jupiter is strong, the person will possess enthusiasm, pride, and ambition. This person would be happy running his or her own business, or managing the business of someone else. He or she would also do well in politics, the church, athletics, or any field where his or her ambitions are given plenty of scope.

You will find few hands with Saturn as the main mount. Someone with this formation will prefer to work on his or her own in a peaceful environment. This person will want to live away from the hustle and bustle of the city. Consequently, he or she would make a good farmer, horticulturist, or landscape gardener. He or she may have an interest in mathematics or engineering and make careers out of these. An interest in the occult could lead to this person making a living as a psychic reader or teacher.

If Apollo is the strongest mount we will have someone who is always positive and happy. He or she will have a quick mind and the ability to work hard to achieve success. This person will be creative and could make a career out of skills in this area. No matter what occupation this person chooses it will in some way reflect his or her love for beauty.

Someone with Mercury as the dominant mount will be shrewd and have good business acumen. If this person is interested in science he or she would make a good doctor or scientist. Law would provide an excellent field for this person's quick brain, ability to work hard, and oratorical skills. In business he or she would be innovative and hard working, always managing to keep several steps ahead of the opposition.

If Venus is the main mount the person will be sympathetic, understanding, and full of energy. He or she will not take life too seriously, and will invariably look upon the bright side. This person would make a good retailer as long as he or she was selling items that were personally liked. The most enthusiastic bookstore owner I have ever met was a striking example of a Venusian. He adored books and considered himself fortunate to be working amongst them. This person would also do well in any philanthropic type field, where his or her sympathy and sense of fair play could be used.

When Mars is the dominant mount you will have someone who is boisterous, aggressive, and courageous. He or she will be adventurous and show great presence of mind in dangerous situations. Naturally, this person would do well in the armed forces, and also could be attracted to police work, security, athletics, and any field offering variety and plenty of excitement.

As Luna governs the imagination, someone with this mount dominant needs to use creativity in his or her career. This person will be good with words, but as he or she lacks confidence, it is more likely to be the written word rather than the spoken. The talents may lie in music, and his or her innate restlessness will be soothed by playing or composing. This person's desire to travel could be well utilized as a travel writer or consultant.

The Fingers

D'Arpentigny, the French army officer who was first to devise a system for classifying palms, was particularly aware of fingers and noticed a striking contrast between the fingers of artists and scientists. Artists, he noticed, generally had smooth fingers, whilst scientists had knotted ones. D'Arpentigny was sufficiently intrigued with his discovery to carry on and become the first "modern" palmist.

People with long fingers are going to be happiest in careers where they can immerse themselves in detail. My bank manager and accountant both have long fingers, something that pleases me greatly as I want them to take great care of my money!

Someone with long, tapering fingers will avoid manual work if at all possible. This person's friend with short, square, or spatulate fingers will be the opposite and will want a "hands-on" job.

Success in Business

You will find self-employed people with every possible variation of hand. A plumber will have a very different hand from a tailor, who likewise will have a different hand from a salesperson.

However, if someone is going to do well in business he or she will have a number of points in common with other successful business people. The first of these is a strong thumb, the larger the better. This gives determination and the desire to succeed.

A good business person will need a destiny line, as this will give direction and focus to his or her life. Occasionally, someone without a destiny line achieves great success, but this is very rare. What will have happened is that this person will have been ambling along quite happily and chanced upon something that led him or her to success. The presence of a destiny line gives the person a road map to follow.

He or she will also need a strong, straight Mercury finger as every business requires communication skills of one sort or another. A long Mercury finger also gives shrewdness and financial acumen.

A good length Jupiter finger will show how ambitious the person is. One person will be content owning a corner delicatessen, whilst another will not rest until he or she has a hundred of them.

As well as this the business person will need the various qualities necessary in the field he or she has chosen. Someone with a broad hand containing few lines, wide apart fingers with spatulate tips, and an angle of practicality on the thumb would last only a few days cooped up in an office. This person needs to be out of doors, and would be happy and successful in careers such as farming or seafaring.

Talents

Fortunately, every one of us is different and I believe that everyone has a talent or special ability of some sort. Usually when we talk of talents we refer to creative abilities, and many people are blessed in this way.

Most people, however, do not do anywhere near as much with their talents as they could. There are a number of reasons for this. The talent may be unrecognized. The talent may not be approved of by the person's family. I once read the palms of a male ballet dancer who did not take up dancing until his twenties because of his father's strong disapproval. Lack of motivation is the main reason people do not develop their talents. I am continually told by clients to whom I have pointed out a talent that they do not have time to work on it. This is simply an excuse. We can all find time to do the things we want to do.

As well, most talents require a sacrifice of some sort. Very few people are prepared to practice the piano for eight hours a day in the hope of ultimately becoming a successful concert pianist. It is the same with athletics. If someone wants to become a champion swimmer he or she is going to have to spend countless hours in the pool swimming up and down whilst friends are out having fun. It requires considerable dedication and plain hard work, no matter how talented the person may be.

Artistic Ability

You are now familiar with the general indications of creativity on the palm. To determine if this creativity is expressed through painting and drawing we look first at the Apollo finger. If this finger is strong, with a good mount at its base and a long first phalange with a broad tip on it, we have someone with ability in this area. A long second phalange will provide a good sense of color. You will always find this sign on people with good taste in clothes.

We also need to check the lower half of the palm to see how imaginative the person is. Ideally, the mount of Luna will be strong, helping to create a curve of creativity on the percussion side of the palm.

If the person wants to be financially successful from art he or she will need a longer than average little finger, a strong thumb, and a reasonably wide palm. If these business indications are absent this person would be better working for others as a staff artist, or perhaps using it as a hobby rather than a career.

Writing Ability

Writing is part of communication and we look first for a good-sized little finger. The second phalange should be the most prominent. If the head line curves up to the mount of Luna the person will be a creative writer with a talent for fiction. If the head line runs straight across the palm the talent will lie more with nonfiction. Fiction writers should have a well-developed lower half of the hand with strong Luna and Venus mounts.

Poets also need a strong sense of rhythm and rhyme, which is indicated by the angle of pitch at the base of the thumb.

Acting Ability

Actors need to express themselves, so a good tip on the Mercury finger is essential. Ideally the fingers should be smooth and tapering to allow the emotions to be expressed. The hand should be as wide as possible to give the person confidence and the ability to push for him or herself. This is very important for long-term success in an extremely difficult field.

Character actors are likely to have knotted fingers. Comedians and actors in comic roles will have well-developed mounts of Mercury and Luna. The whole percussion side of the hand should be well marked.

Musical Ability

An entire book could be written on determining the different types of musical talent in the hand, which makes it hard to even attempt a few lines on the subject.

Singing ability is indicated by perfectly round fingers and a thumb containing both the angles of practicality and pitch. A good size mount of Venus gives a love of melody, and the Luna mount harmony. For success in this field the person should also have a good length Apollo finger and a pronounced Apollo mount.

To be successful as a player of a musical instrument the person will need the angles of practicality and pitch, plus strong Venus and Luna mounts. Successful instrumentalists can be found with every possible shape of hand, though players of stringed instruments are usually possessors of air and water hands. Players of percussion instruments usually have earth hands with broad fingertips.

In addition, talented musicians are likely to have a loop of music, loop of response, or loop of stringed music.

Dancing Ability

Dancers need to be able to respond to rhythm and time, making the two angles of practicality and pitch essential. The life line needs to come well across a preferably wide palm, giving stamina and energy. Venus and Luna mounts should be high and firm, enabling the person to lose him or herself in the dance.

A jazz dancer is likely to have pointed or conic fingertips, emphasizing inspiration and the ability to improvise. A dancer with square tips will be able to do exactly what is required and will perform previously memorized steps perfectly.

CHAPTER
TWENTY-FOUR

Putting It
All Together

TRY AND LOOK AT as many different hands as
you can. The more hands you look at, the
quicker you will become at recognizing the
main features. Start by giving very brief readings to friends and acquaintances. As your confidence and knowledge increase you will
gradually be able to lengthen your readings.

I always read hands in a set order. This
ensures that I do not accidentally leave something out. I begin with the person's major hand,
determining the shape, and in the process note
how firm or soft the hand is, and how much

hair is on the back. I also determine which of the mounts is predominant. I then look at the heart line, head line, and life line, in that order. Along the way I also examine the girdle of Venus, sister lines, and any other lines that are involved with the main lines I am looking at. After the life line, I examine the destiny line, thumb, and fingers before checking out financial potential and travel. I then look at the the mounts and minor markings on the hand. Finally, I check for any dermatoglyphic loops that I may not have covered in the course of the reading. The process is repeated with the minor hand. As I examine the palm I automatically confirm my evaluation by checking indications in other parts of the palm. For instance,

if I saw someone with a writer's fork on their head line I would immediately look at the second phalange of the Mercury finger to see if the writer's fork could be used for creative writing, or whether it simply meant the person came up with good ideas that could be made practical. Again, I automatically look at the person's mount of Venus while examining the heart line as both are involved with the person's love life. After checking in this way, I return to where I was and carry on.

Here is a sample reading given for a thirty-year-old man (24a):

"You have a good strong hand. If you mentally take the fingers and thumb off, you are left with a perfect square. This makes you a practical, down-to-earth sort of person, someone who can tackle anything and do pretty well with it.

"You need to be busy and on the go all the time. You can see the whole situation at a glance and tend to get impatient with people who take all day. You like to get in, get the job done, and get out again, rather than have something that goes on and on.

"Your heart line is strong and clear. It has a nice curve to it and it ultimately ends in the perfect spot between these two fingers. That makes for a warm and loving relationship that builds and grows with time. You have had a few ups and downs in this area of your life.

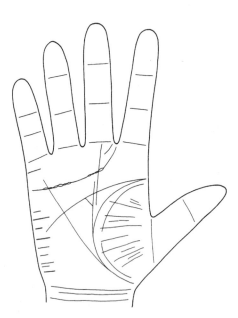

24a. Palm of thirty-year-old man

These little islands indicate those periods and, fortunately, the bulk of them are behind you. We all have ups and downs at times, of course, and you are no exception, but the ones ahead are very minor compared with the past. This little line here means that you won't be lonely in your old age, something some people do worry about.

"You have a strong head line. It curves up into the creative subconscious part of your hand, so you have a good imagination. It is important that any work you do at any stage has plenty of variety to it, as otherwise you would lose interest very quickly.

"This fork here is called a 'writer's fork.'"It doesn't necessarily mean writing, but it does show that you can come up with a good idea and then turn it around and make it real. You have the ability to make your thoughts practical. This is very useful and you should pay serious attention to your ideas.

"You are inclined to be cautious, which is good. You don't jump into things. You feel the water first, and then proceed. You have always been like this, and you also tend to hold part of yourself back, which is a sort of protection. You are not quite as trusting as you have been.

"Your life line is a particularly long one. It comes well across your palm,

and this gives you great stamina and staying power. If you are doing something you enjoy, you can go on and on indefinitely. These little lines are called worry lines. You have your share of those, at times. You worry when there is cause to worry, rather than being a worrier as such.

"You have what is called a sister line inside your life line. It is called that as it is sister to the life line and protects it. It is a bit like having two life lines. Things that would affect other people physically will not affect you to the same extent.

"Your physical fitness seems to fluctuate at times, but you usually look after yourself and you will still be physically active in your old age.

"Your destiny line starts inside your life line. This makes for a strong family influence on you early on in life. Someone had a very powerful influence on you when you were very young, and this remains. It looks as if, at the moment, you are reevaluating things. Your destiny line has paused, and it starts again in a slightly new direction. You may feel a bit confused or frustrated just at the moment. This is very temporary, and once you start moving forward again you won't even know yourself. The new path is stronger than the old and gives you better opportunities.

"You have a strong thumb. If people approach you the right way, you are very easy to get on with. If they rub you up the wrong way, you very quickly dig in your heels. You can be stubborn when the opportunity demands it. This is good, as it means that people cannot take advantage of you.

"You have a little bit more logic than willpower. This means that you come up with great ideas but don't always get around to doing them. You may need to give yourself a push at times.

"You have a good length little finger. The tip section of it is very long, so your forté would be in some form of verbal communication. Selling, for instance, would allow you to develop your skills in this area.

"You have good taste, and actually would do very well if you were selling something that you personally found to be attractive.

"You have quite a bit of drive and ambition. If you want something, you are prepared to get out there and work hard for it. You won't stop until you have succeeded. You should aim as high as you can. This drive and ambition is good, but you must make sure to pause and relax every now and again.

"You have a secure money sign. It is an indication that you will ultimately do pretty well financially, but it comes about through a great deal of hard work and effort. You are good with it once you get it, also. With hard work and good money management you will eventually be quite comfortably off.

"Your health line is good and strong. You have a good sound constitution, and as long as you keep yourself reasonably fit, you will enjoy good health.

"There is quite a bit of travel shown on your hand. Some of it is just day-dreaming, but the reality is there as well. There is even some travel very late in life, so it is not something you ever tire of doing.

"You have just the one main line of romantic attachment. This means there is one really important relationship that builds and grows, and is still there in your old age. There were probably a number of girlfriends in the past, but over a lifetime, just one is of any account. That makes you a very fortunate person.

"You have a good hand and, once you get going in this new direction, there will be no stopping you."

Did you see all the markings on his hand to indicate the different things I said? If not, here are the main points mentioned.

Everything in the first paragraph is said because he has a square-shaped palm. The second paragraph is derived entirely from his short fingers.

The third paragraph is related to his heart line. I begin by commenting that it is "strong and clear." This is because the line is clearly visible on the palm, denoting vitality and energy. He has a physical heart line that ends between the Jupiter and Saturn fingers, enabling me to say, "It has a nice curve to it and it ultimately ends in the perfect space between these two fingers." I then indicate and give the meanings of the islands on the line, and finally mention the short line at the end of the heart line "that means you won't be lonely in your old age."

I then move on to describe his imaginative head line. I comment on and explain the writer's fork, and conclude this line by telling him he is inclined to be cautious, because his life line and head lines join at the start.

I then mention the length of his life line and how far across the palm it comes. I explain the meanings of the worry lines and sister line. The paragraph on physical fitness relates to the quality of the life line at different points in the person's life. This is not easy to illustrate on a drawing. Ideally, the life line should be clear and reasonably deep. The periods when the quality of the line change indicate times when the person's physical fitness fluctuates.

I explain the strong family influence derived from his destiny line starting inside the life line. I then explain how he is reevaluating his life. This information comes from the change of direction in his destiny line.

When I say, "You have a strong thumb," I press against it to see how stubborn and rigid he is. Obviously, this man's thumb is very strong and does not bend back when pressed. I comment on his second phalange being longer than the first, giving him more logic than willpower.

Now I move on to the fingers, and begin by commenting on the tip phalange of his Mercury finger. The next paragraph talks about his good taste, which is derived from a good middle phalange of his Apollo finger. I comment on how he would be good at selling things that he personally liked because a good tip on the Mercury finger and a strong middle phalange on Apollo relate to this.

The next paragraph ("You have quite a bit of drive and ambition") relates to the length and quality of his Jupiter finger. My comments on ambition are made because his Jupiter finger is longer than his Apollo finger.

The next paragraph relates to money and is derived from the fact that his money triangle at the intersection of his destiny and head lines is of a good size and is also a complete triangle.

He has a hepatica, or health line, so I comment on this. I always have a look at the person's life line as well when checking the hepatica, as this shows the amount of vitality and energy available.

I then look at his travel lines. Some of these are clear and well defined, but others are fainter and rather indistinct. This is why I say, "Some of it is just daydreaming, but the reality is there as well."

Finally, I comment on his line of romantic attachment. I would have noticed this line immediately, but have not mentioned it until now in case other factors on the hand affected his relationships.

I conclude with a final paragraph that is intended to be positive and encouraging.

Here is another reading, this time for a woman in her early forties (24b):

"You are naturally intuitive. You seem to feel things all the time, and your hunches would invariably be correct.

"You are at an interesting point in your life as things are starting to come right for you. You have certainly had your share of ups and downs emotionally, but most of those are behind you. They have colored the way you look at the world, of course, but you have not become cynical or bitter.

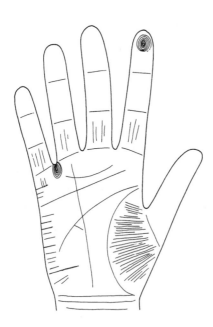

24b. Palm of woman in her early forties

"You have what is called a mental heart line. This means that you like people, but also like a bit of room around you. Although you feel things so deeply, you probably found it hard to express your innermost feelings early on in life. That has gradually become easier over the years.

"You are very sensitive, and people have been able to hurt you at times, maybe even without knowing it. This has not made life easy, but you have learned to control it. If you are doing something creative you could channel these energies, but in daily life it has been a real nuisance.

"You are also rather idealistic and people have let you down at times, or maybe not lived up to expectations. Fortunately, you no longer expect perfection.

"You have a clear, well-marked head line running all the way up to this quadrant of your palm, which governs the imagination. You have an excellent imagination, and it is important that whatever job you do at any time is stimulating and varied, as otherwise you would float off into another world very quickly.

"There is a tendency to jump into things at times. You can be very impulsive. Also, you are gradually becoming more and more outspoken the older you get. This is bound to get you into hot water at times, but at least people know where they stand!

"You have a long, clear life line. You don't always have the energy you would like, and you probably need plenty of rest to recharge. Your main enemy is worry, and it looks as if you are pretty good at that! Most of that is family worry.

"Your destiny line starts well away from your life line, so you have enjoyed being independent right from the moment you were born. It is a very straight, direct line, so speaking generally, you usually know where you are going. The only problem is you normally want everything today, rather than when it does happen.

"You have a strong thumb and can certainly stand up for yourself. You can be extremely stubborn when necessary.

"You have a good length little finger. This finger governs communication, and you have a large middle section. This means that you can express yourself well with words on paper. It may sometimes be easier to write something down than to say it out loud. You could very easily develop your writing talents, if you wished.

"Your ring finger is a good length. The strong middle section gives you a natural good taste. Unfortunately, your Saturn finger curves over the Apollo finger. Saturn governs restrictions and means

that subconsciously you hold yourself back creatively. If you were to do something creative it would be of a higher standard than you yourself would realise.

"Your first finger is long and straight. This means that you have leadership potential and invariably manage to get your own way in the end. You should always aim as high as you can, as you always get there in the end.

"You have a great deal of originality in this finger. Everything you do has your own definite stamp on it. If you took on a job that has been done in a certain way for the last fifty years, within a week or two you would be doing it in your own particular way.

"You will ultimately develop a very strong faith of some sort. It may or may not be a church-type religion, but whatever it is it will ultimately play a major part in your life. You have double intuition lines, so could easily get premonitions in the form of dreams. You seem to be highly attuned and very intuitive, and appear to use this in every area of your life. If you had a major decision to make and logic told you to go in one direction, whilst your intuition indicated another path, you should always go with your intuition.

"You have some strain lines on your fingers. This means it is time to have a few days off, or a bit of a break, if possible. Fortunately, there are no stress lines on your hand.

"You have an open money sign. This means that money comes in, but a great deal of it manages to escape again very quickly. You will always be good at spending money!

"Some of that money will be spent on travel. It looks as if you enjoy all of the travel you do, and you will even be doing some travelling in your old age. It is not something you ever tire of. There is quite a bit of daydreaming about travel, but the reality is there as well.

"You need a great deal of excitement and stimulation in your life, something to look forward to. Travel is just one of the ways in which you satisfy this need. You will do a number of amazing things in your life, and could well be a real embarrassment to your grandchildren! However, you will still be enjoying life.

"You have a unique sense of humor, a sense of the ridiculous. It is a bit off-beat, but has been a saving grace at times. It is good to be able to laugh.

"You have three major lines of romantic attachment, indicating the possibility of three men in your life. However, of the three only one is really important. Children lines are very hard to gauge these days, because of contraceptives, but you have three strong lines there.

"You have certainly had to work hard to get where you have. You are not the same person you used to be. Nothing worthwhile is ever achieved without a great deal of hard work and persistence. You are on the right track now and have the potential to create a highly stimulating and rewarding future for yourself."

Normally, a reading of this sort is a conversation, rather than a monologue, which enables you to cover the specific areas the client needs help with in more depth.

You will have noticed that I have concentrated on the positive aspects of the person's life, rather than the negative. If I was giving a full-length reading, which would last about an hour, I would cover more of the negative traits, but the reading would still be as positive as possible. I want my clients to leave feeling that they can overcome their problems and limitations and lead successful, happy lives. There is no excuse for sending someone away feeling as if they want to jump off the nearest tall building.

I see myself as advising and guiding my clients by showing them areas where they can progress. My job is to help them and to give them hope. Obviously, I must include negative aspects as well to give balance. No one is perfect.

With these two readings I have looked at just one palm. In practice, I would read both the major hand, to see what the person was doing with their life, and the minor hand, to see inherited traits, potentials, and what the person was thinking about.

CHAPTER TWENTY-FIVE

Making Prints

It is very helpful to build up a collection of people's palm prints for a number of reasons. First, as you continue your study and research into palmistry you will be able to refer back to your growing collection of prints.

It will also make you more fully aware of how diverse people's hands really are. You will gradually discover, for instance, that most people with earth hands have comparatively few lines on their palms, whilst people with water hands usually have a large number.

If you take the prints of a few generations of the same family you will be able to trace different combinations that run through a family. You will also be able to see whether someone inherited their musical abilities from their mother or father, or maybe from a grandparent.

Also, you will be able to see how people's hands change over a period of time. I find it fascinating when someone returns for another appointment to compare the print of the hand now with the print taken at a previous visit. It makes it very clear how people change, develop, and move forward—or backward!

A number of health factors can be seen more easily by looking at a print, rather than the palm. For instance, the first sign of cancer is indicated by a breakdown of the skin ridges on the palm. This is not always possible to determine without a print. Health factors in the palm are beyond the scope of this book, but it is an area that is being studied by more and more scientists around the world. At the Kennedy-Galton Centre attached to the University of London, scientists have been studying palms since the 1940s, and are gradually verifying scientifically facts that palm readers have known for hundreds, if not thousands, of years.

Taking a Print

Obtain a supply of good quality bond paper at least eight-and-a-half-by-eleven inches in size. You will also need a tube of artist's water-based black ink. Artists use these for lino prints, and you will find a tube of ink at any artists' supply house. At the same place you will be able to buy an ink roller about four inches wide.

You will also need a slightly spongy surface to put the paper on. I use a one-inch stack of tea towels that have been folded in half. Initially, I used a large oblong of soft rubber that had previously supported an old-fashioned typewriter. It does not matter what the surface is, just as long as it has some give in it, as this enables you to take a print of the hollow of the palm.

Arrange your stack of tea towels, or whatever, and place one sheet of paper on top.

Squeeze out a small amount of ink, either on to a small piece of glass, or a spare piece of paper. Roll it with the roller until it is smooth and the roller has a fine, even surface of ink on it.

Ask the person whose prints you are taking to remove any rings they may be wearing, if it

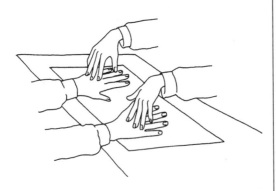

25a. Making a palm print

is possible, and then hold both palms out. With long even strokes of the roller, cover the palms with a fine coating of ink.

Tell this person to hold their hands naturally and to then place both hands simultaneously onto the sheet of paper (25a). Once the hands are on the paper press down gently on the back of each palm to ensure that the center of the palm makes an impression on the paper (25b, 25c). Hold down each end of the paper and ask your client to raise both hands straight up in the air. Once this has been done, take a separate print of both thumbs, as you record only the side of the thumb whilst printing the palms. Usually I take two sets of prints as my clients like to have a copy for themselves.

If your client has a particularly high mount of Venus and/or Luna you will find it difficult to get a complete impression. With these people I ask them to raise both hands slowly into the air, whilst still attached to the paper. I then gently press the paper into the hollow of their palms.

With a little bit of practice you will get perfect prints almost every time. You may find you prefer to take prints of the hands separately. I personally like to have them both on the same piece of paper, but it is much easier to do one at a time.

As the ink is water-based, your client will be able to wash the ink off easily with soap and water whilst you examine the prints.

Water-based ink is the easiest material to work with, but a number of other things will do if it is not available. Lipstick makes excellent prints. Fingerprint ink is excellent, but not always easy to obtain. Oil-based ink is good, but can be difficult for your client to remove. In the past I have also used an ink pad used for rubber stamps, and Gestetner ink.

Photocopiers do an excellent job of capturing the lines and skin ridge patterns, but be aware that the actual shape of the hand can change slightly as the person presses their palms on to the glass.

I always identify and date the print. On a separate sheet of paper I record any comments I wish to make about the palm. This is deliberate as I may not wish my client to see my notes.

You will find that your growing collection of palm prints will become more and more useful for you as you continue your studies in the fascinating field of palmistry.

25b. Correctly made hand print, left hand

25d. Incorrectly made hand print, left hand

25c. Correctly made hand print, right hand

25e. Incorrectly made hand print, right hand

CHAPTER
TWENTY-SIX

Conclusion

I HOPE YOU have found this book helpful and interesting. Palmistry is a subject I have been fascinated with for almost all of my life and I hope my enthusiasm has come across in every page.

By now you should be well on the way to becoming a competent palmist, and I hope to have the pleasure of having you read my hands sometime in the not-so-distant future. In the meantime, read as much as you can about palmistry and look at as many hands as you can. You will be amazed at the insights you will gain about other people, even when simply glimpsing their hands. Start with short readings. Tell people that you are still learning, so they will not expect too much from you at first. Be kind and caring. When you are giving readings you have the power to influence people greatly. Be gentle and think before you speak.

On the next page is a list of suggested reading. I recommend all of these books, but particularly the ones by Andrew Fitzherbert, David Brandon-Jones, and Elizabeth Brenner.

SUGGESTED READING

Nathaniel Altman, *The Palmistry Workbook,* Northamptonshire, U.K.: Aquarian Press, 1984.

Nathaniel Altman and Andrew Fitzherbert, *Career, Success and Self-Fulfilment,* Northamptonshire, U.K.: Aquarian Press, 1988.

Mir Bashir, *The Art of Hand Analysis,* London: Frederick Muller Limited, 1973.

William G. Benham, *The Laws of Scientific Handreading,* New York: Duell, Sloan and

Pearce, 1900. Recently republished as *The Benham Book of Palmistry,* Van Nuys, Calif.: Newcastle Publishing.

David Brandon-Jones, *Practical Palmistry,* London: Rider and Company, 1981.

Elizabeth Brenner, *The Hand Book,* Millbrae, Calif.: Celestial Arts, 1980.

Elizabeth Brenner, *Hand in Hand,* Millbrae, Calif.: Celestial Arts, 1981.

Andrew Fitzherbert, *Hand Psychology,* London: Angus and Robertson, 1986.

Fred Gettings, *The Book of the Hand,* London: Paul Hamlyn, 1965.

Judith Hipskind, *Palmistry, the Whole View,* St. Paul, Minn.: Llewellyn Publications, 1977.

Beryl Hutchinson, *Your Life in Your Hands,* London: Neville Spearman, 1967.

INDEX

A

REACH FOR THE MOON

Llewellyn publishes hundreds of books on your favorite subjects!
To get these exciting books, including the ones on the following pages,
check your local bookstore or order them directly from Llewellyn.

Order by Phone
- Call toll-free within the U.S. and Canada, 1-800-THE MOON
- In Minnesota, call (651) 291-1970
- We accept VISA, MasterCard, and American Express

Order by Mail
- Send the full price of your order (MN residents add 7% sales tax)
  in U.S. funds, plus postage & handling to:

  Llewellyn Worldwide
  P.O. Box 64383, Dept. 1-56718-790-0
  St. Paul, MN 55164–0383, U.S.A.

Postage & Handling
- **Standard** (U.S., Mexico, & Canada)

If your order is:
$20.00 or under, add $5.00
$20.01–$100.00, add $6.00
Over $100, shipping is free

(Continental U.S. orders ship UPS. AK, HI, PR, & P.O. Boxes ship USPS 1st class. Mex. & Can. ship PMB.)

- **Second Day Air** (Continental U.S. only): $10.00 for one book + $1.00
  per each additional book
- **Express** (AK, HI, & PR only) [Not available for P.O. Box delivery. For
  street address delivery only.]: $15.00 for one book + $1.00 per each
  additional book
- **International Surface Mail:** Add $1.00 per item
- **International Airmail:** Books—Add the retail price of each item;
  Non-book items—Add $5.00 per item

Please allow 4–6 weeks for delivery on all orders.
Postage and handling rates subject to change.

Discounts
We offer a 20% discount to group leaders or agents. You must order a
minimum of 5 copies of the same book to get our special quantity price.

Free Catalog

Get a free copy of our color catalog, *New Worlds of Mind and Spirit*.
Subscribe for just $10.00 in the United States and Canada ($30.00
overseas, airmail). Many bookstores carry *New Worlds*—ask for it!

Visit our website at www.llewellyn.com for more information.

Palm Reading for Beginners
Find the Future in the Palm of Your Hand

Richard Webster

Announce in any gathering that you read palms and you will be surrounded by people thrilled to show you their hands. When you have finished *Palm Reading for Beginners,* you will be able to look at anyone's palm (including your own) and confidently and effectively tell them about their personality, love life, hidden talents, career options, prosperity, and health.

Palmistry is possibly the oldest of the occult sciences, with principles that have not changed in 2,600 years. This step-by-step guide clearly explains the basics, as well as advanced research conducted in the past few years on such subjects as dermatoglyphics.

Now you can learn to read palms even if you have no prior knowledge of the subject:

- Determine someone's predisposition toward certain illnesses
- Gain knowledge from the shape and texture of a hand, its major lines and minor lines, timing on the lines, and the fingers
- Learn what telling information is on the mounts, quadrangles, marks on the hand, skin ridge patterns, and signs of health, wealth, and happiness
- Learn how to conduct honest yet sensitive readings

1-56718-791-9
264 pp., 5³⁄₁₆ x 8, illus. $9.95

To order, call 1-800-THE MOON

Aura Reading for Beginners
Develop Your Psychic Awareness for Health & Success

RICHARD WEBSTER

When you lose your temper, don't be surprised if a dirty red haze suddenly appears around you. If you do something magnanimous, your aura will expand. Now you can learn to see the energy that emanates off yourself and other people through the proven methods taught by Richard Webster in his psychic training classes.

Learn to feel the aura, see the colors in it, and interpret what those colors mean. Explore the chakra system, and how to restore balance to chakras that are over- or under-stimulated. Then you can begin to imprint your desires into your aura to attract what you want in your life.

These proven methods for seeing the aura will help you:

- Interpret the meanings of colors in the aura
- Find a career that is best suited for you
- Enjoy excellent health
- Discover areas of your life that you need to work on
- Imprint what you want in your future into your aura
- Make aura portraits with pastels or colored pencils
- Discover the signs of impending ill health, drug abuse, and pain
- See what the next few weeks or months are going to be like for you

1-56718-798-6
208 pp., 5³⁄₁₆ x 8, illus. $9.95

To order, call 1-800-THE MOON
Prices subject to change without notice

Astral Travel for Beginners
Transcend Time and Space with Out-of-Body Experiences

RICHARD WEBSTER

Astral projection, or the out-of-body travel, is a completely natural experience. You have already astral traveled thousands of times in your sleep, you just don't remember it when you wake up. Now, you can learn how to leave your body at will, be fully conscious of the experience, and remember it when you return.

The exercises in this book are carefully graded to take you step-by-step through an actual out-of-body experience. Once you have accomplished this, it becomes easier and easier to leave your body. That's why the emphasis in this book is on your first astral travel. By the time you have finished the exercises in this book you will be able to leave your body and explore the astral realms with confidence and total safety:

- Keep an eye on loved ones and friends
- Instantly visit any place in the world that you desire
- Transport yourself back or forward through time
- Lose all fear of death

1-56718-796-X
256 pp., 5³⁄₁₆ x 8 $9.95

To order, call 1-800-THE MOON
Prices subject to change without notice

101 Feng Shui Tips for the Home
RICHARD WEBSTER

For thousand of years, people in the Far East have used feng shui to improve their home and family lives and live in harmony with the earth. Certainly, people who practice feng-shui achieve a deep contentment that is denied most others. They usually do well romantically and financially. Architects around the world are beginning to incorporate the concepts of feng shui into their designs. Even people like Donald Trump freely admit to using feng shui.

Watch your success and spirits soar when you discover:
- How to evaluate the current feng shui energy in your home
- What to do about negative energy coming from neighbors
- How to use fountains or aquariums to attract money
- The best position for the front door
- Where to place your stove for the best effect on the food you serve
- The best color to paint your kitchen
- Where to sit your dinner guests to encourage a friendly atmosphere
- How to arrange your living room furniture
- Colors to use and avoid for each member of the family

1-56718-809-5
192 pp., 5 x 8, charts

$9.95

Feng Shui For Love & Romance
RICHARD WEBSTER

For thousands of years, the Chinese have known that if they arrange their homes and possessions in the right way, they will attract positive energy into their life, including a life rich in love and friendship. Now you can take advantage of this ancient knowledge so you can attract the right partner to you; if you're currently in a relationship, you can strengthen the bond between you and your beloved.

It's amazingly simple and inexpensive. Want your partner to start listening to you? Display some yellow flowers in the *Ken* (communication) area of your home. Do you want to bring more friends of both sexes into your life? Place some green plants or candles in the *Chien* (friendship) area. Is your relationship good in most respects but lacking passion between the sheets? Be forewarned—once you activate this area with feng shui, you may have problems getting enough sleep at night!

1-56718-792-7
192 pp., 5¼ x 8

$9.95

Soul Mates
Understanding Relationships Across Time

RICHARD WEBSTER

The eternal question: how do you find your soul mate—that special, magical person with whom you have spent many previous incarnations? Popular metaphysical author Richard Webster explores every aspect of the soul mate phenomenon in his newest release.

The incredible soul mate connection allows you and your partner to progress even further with your souls' growth and development with each incarnation. *Soul Mates* begins by explaining reincarnation, karma, and the soul, and prepares you to attract your soul mate to you. After reading examples of soul mates from the author's own practice, and famous soul mates from history, you will learn how to recall your past lives. In addition, you will gain valuable tips on how to strengthen your relationship so it grows stronger and better as time goes by.

1-56718-789-7
216 pp., 6 x 9 $12.95

To order, call 1-800-THE MOON
Prices subject to change without notice

Seven Secrets to Success
A Story of Hope

RICHARD WEBSTER

Originally written as a letter from the author to his suicidal friend, this inspiring little book has been photocopied, passed along from person to person, and even appeared on the internet without the author's permission. Now available in book form, this underground classic offers hope to the weary and motivation for us all to let go of the past and follow our dreams.

It is the story of Kevin, who at the age of twenty-eight is on the verge of suicide after the failure of his business and his marriage. Then he meets Todd Melvin, an elderly gentleman with a mysterious past. As their friendship unfolds, Todd teaches Kevin seven secrets—secrets that can give you the power to turn your life around, begin anew, and reap success beyond your wildest dreams.

1-56718-797-8
144 pp., 5³⁄₁₆ x 8 $6.95

To order, call 1-800-THE MOON
Prices subject to change without notice

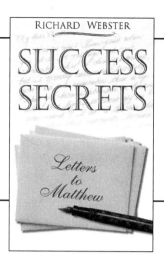

RICHARD WEBSTER

SUCCESS SECRETS

Letters to Matthew

**Success Secrets:
Letters to Matthew**
RICHARD WEBSTER

Rekindle your passion for your life's work.

Matthew is lacking vision and passion in his life. His marriage is on the rocks and his boss is worried about Matthew's falling sales figures. Just as he is feeling the lowest he has felt in years, he goes to his mailbox and finds an envelope addressed to him, with no return address and no stamp. He instantly recognizes the handwriting as that of his old history teacher from high school. Wouldn't Mr. Nevin be dead by now? Why would Matthew get a letter from him after thirty years?

The letter and the others that follow are the backbone of this little book. Each one gives Matthew encouragement and new ways to deal with his life.

This little book is a quick read about following your dreams, setting goals, overcoming obstacles, pushing yourself even further, and making work fun.

Don't lead a half-life, Matthew. I'm trying to help you find your passion. When you find your passion you'll never work again. Of course, you'll probably work extremely hard, but it won't seem like work. And then, if you win millions of dollars, you'll carry on with whatever it is you are doing. Because it is your passion, your purpose, your reason for being here.

1-56718-788-9
168 pp., 5³⁄₁₆ x 8 $7.95

To order, call 1-800-THE MOON
Prices subject to change without notice

Spirit Guides & Angel Guardians
Contact Your Invisible Helpers

RICHARD WEBSTER

They come to our aid when we least expect it, and they disappear as soon as their work is done. Invisible helpers are available to all of us; in fact, we all regularly receive messages from our guardian angels and spirit guides but usually fail to recognize them. This book will help you to realize when this occurs. And when you carry out the exercises provided, you will be able to communicate freely with both your guardian angels and spirit guides.

- Learn the important differences between a guardian angel and a spirit guide
- Invoke the Archangels for help in achieving your goals
- Discover the different ways your guardian angel speaks to you
- Create your own guardian angel from within
- Use your guardian angel to aid in healing yourself and others
- Enhance your creativity by calling on angelic assistance
- Find your life's purpose through your guardian angel
- Use time-tested methods to contact your spirit guides
- Use your spirit guides to help you release negative emotions
- Call on specific guides for nurturing, support, fun, motivation, and wisdom
- Visit your guides through past-life regression

1-56718-795-1
368 pp., 5 ³⁄₁₆ x 8
Also available in Spanish

$9.95

To order, call 1-800-THE MOON
Prices subject to change without notice